Women and Transition

Women and Transition

Reinventing Work and Life

Linda Rossetti

palgrave
macmillan

First published in 2015 by
PALGRAVE MACMILLAN®
in the United States—a division of St. Martin's Press LLC,
175 Fifth Avenue, New York, NY 10010.

Where this book is distributed in the UK, Europe and the rest of the world,
this is by Palgrave Macmillan, a division of Macmillan Publishers Limited,
registered in England, company number 785998, of Houndmills,
Basingstoke, Hampshire RG21 6XS.

Palgrave Macmillan is the global academic imprint of the above companies
and has companies and representatives throughout the world.

Palgrave® and Macmillan® are registered trademarks in the United States,
the United Kingdom, Europe and other countries.

ISBN: 978–1–137–47654–8

Library of Congress Cataloging-in-Publication Data

Rossetti, Linda.
    Women & transition : reinventing work and life / Linda Rossetti.
       pages cm
    Includes bibliographical references and index.
    ISBN 978–1–137–47654–8 (alk. paper)
      1. Career changes. 2. Women—Employment. 3. Work and family.
    4. Work-life balance. 5. Career development. I. Title.
    II. Title: Women and transition.

HF5384.R67 2015
650.1082—dc23   2015016048

A catalogue record of the book is available from the British Library.

Design by Newgen Knowledge Works (P) Ltd., Chennai, India.

First edition: October 2015

10 9 8 7 6 5 4 3 2

Printed in the United States of America.

Dedicated to j, w, and s

Contents

Figures

Introduction

I did not start out by sitting down to write a book about transition. I began by trying to reconcile a disconnect I experienced between society's characterization of women's progress and what I felt and experienced on the ground. There was a gap, an undeniable gap, between the narrative of women's progress and what I saw all around me. While I had been immune to this gap for a long time, an experience that began in my mid-forties caused me to look deeper into what was going on with me and with women more broadly. Thanks to that inquiry, I found transition.

I remember the first day of my transition vividly. It was January. I was unglued because it was the first time I had stepped away from a fast-paced, always-on career that had spanned more than 20 years. My first instinct was to establish some familiarity. I set up an improvised work area in my basement's laundry room. Truth be told, I escaped to the basement after realizing that my in-home office was useless. The happy squeals of my then very young children reverberated throughout the house. The basement was the only quiet refuge. An old wooden barstool served as my chair. A folding table stood in nicely as a makeshift desk. It was a bit musty, but overall functional. It would do. I had two consulting gigs to start. Time to begin.

As I acclimated to my surroundings that morning, I turned on my computer and started with the headlines of the day's news. Everywhere I turned the media was celebrating women's progress. Even though the numbers were small, in all cases the media blanketed its coverage with a vocabulary of success. I am sure you have seen some flavor of these annual headlines. The often-quoted statistics include women's participation rates in leadership or executive ranks across industry; their representation in meaningful structures in our society like Congress or the Supreme Court; or their inclusion in exclusive clubs, like among the ranks of the world's wealthiest in the *Forbes* Annual List of Billionaires.

The world featured in the news that day seemed a million miles away from my basement. I could not help but wonder what, if anything, these statistics told me about the woman who worked around the corner, about my colleagues from my previous job, and about my friends—some of whom were single, some of whom choose to stay home with children, and others of whom choose to pursue their careers amid ever-changing family needs. I found myself wondering about the gap between the two camps: the one celebrated in the media and the one represented by the women all around me. The women in both camps were smart, engaging, and highly motivated individuals. All were capable of making extraordinary contributions in whatever they chose. Why did those statistics feel so distant?

In the five years since that morning, I have concluded that these statistics tell us "very little" about women's progress. Instead, I have learned an incredible amount about women's progress from transition. My reactions that morning inspired me to push aside the consulting work and ask myself some hard questions about my experience and the experience of other women. That query serves as the baseline of this book.

Women and Transition: Reinventing Work and Life introduces women to a framework for understanding transition and offers a practical toolkit for those who choose to pursue transition in their own lives. The book's objective is twofold: to increase women's awareness of transition, and to support women in successfully transitioning. The book relies on my own experience, along with the experiences of hundreds of other women who shared their transition stories with me.

Why Do I tell This Story?

I am deeply committed to transition, thanks to the enormous gifts I have derived from navigating it. There are four reasons why *I* want to tell this story: my lack of preparedness when I found myself in transition; my interest in addressing what I observed; the research I conducted as a means of figuring transition out; and my belief in the importance of the topic to women broadly. Together, these reasons also informed how I chose to tell the story.

I arrived at transition at 45, nearly ready to keel over. My husband and I had our first child when I was 39, and our second only sixteen months later when I was 40. I spent most of the next five years in a demanding high-pressure job as Executive Vice President of Human Resources and Administration for Iron Mountain, a Fortune 500 company with over 21,000 employees in 37 countries. I landed the job never having worked in human resources (HR) before because of well-developed networks that I always maintained. I was recruited by a former colleague of mine who would serve as the company's CEO during most of my tenure. He wanted a business person to run HR and help him transform the company. From a purely professional lens, I could not have described a more exciting challenge. Did I mention that when I had children, I never considered not working? This fast-paced period when my children were toddlers was consistent with my career up until that moment. I graduated with an MBA from the Harvard Business School. I started and served as CEO of a venture capital-backed technology services company in the late 1990s that was later acquired by Perot Systems, Inc. My former colleague and then boss at Iron Mountain had served on the Advisory Board of the tech start-up that I ran. On top of all this, I arrived at transition having achieved nearly all of the career goals that I had set out for myself. It was no wonder that I had no idea what transition was all about.

The second reason I want to tell this story is that I was surprised when I found little information available to help me understand why, despite all this success, I struggled to reconcile competing interests in my life. Something was not right. Like many of us facing change, I arrived at transition hoping to find a resource or even some vocabulary to help me navigate what was unfamiliar terrain. Nothing available seemed to explain what I was experiencing.

Even more surprising, I met many, many other women who felt the same. Their stories were different, their experiences hailed from a broad set of circumstances, but their feelings were the same. A little lost, disoriented, with no compass to help point them in the right direction, or any direction for that matter, some of these women were re-engaging in the workforce after a prolonged absence or exiting the full-time workforce in response to escalating family or elder-care needs. Others were searching for a new reality postdivorce or exploring new career options after realizing their current track was not all that engaging. While it was comforting to know these women existed, I was shocked at the cone of silence that engulfed their experience. No one talked about this.

Through listening to all of these women's varied stories, I learned a great deal about women's transitions. I also encountered patterns within transitions that no one else seemed to even think about. Women in seemingly different situations shared with me remarkably similar experiences about transition. None of the reading I had done discussed this pattern. A woman in the throes of a divorce. Another re-engaging in the workplace after a prolonged absence. Despite differences in these two experiences, I heard a lot of similarities. I wondered what to make of it.

The third reason I wanted to share this story is linked to how I reacted when I could not find relevant information that mirrored my experience. I initiated my own research. At first, it took the form of a blog, called Novofemina.com. The name combined two Latin words: *novo*, meaning "renewal," and *femina*, meaning "woman." I was thrilled to use the blog to engage other women in a conversation about transition. It was great, but it was not enough. I wanted to learn more. This desire led me to conduct more research in hopes of gaining a broader understanding of transition. It included an online survey, focus groups, expert panels, and one-on-one interviews. In total, more than 200 individuals participated in the research. While this sample may not be representative of all women, it gave me tremendous insight into transition and the patterns that accompany its phases.

The last reason I wanted to tell this story is that I wanted to share what I learned about transition with other women. By transferring my learnings, I hope that transition becomes accessible for any woman who chooses it.

While these reasons convinced me that there was a story to tell, they also informed how I choose to tell this story. While I often use my own experience as a storyline for this book, the book is far from a recitation of my work experiences or the antics I observed while working at elite levels in organizations. I consider myself incredibly fortunate to have worked and contributed in this manner. But those experiences are not this story. This story is my transition story and the story of women who shared their transition perspectives with me. It is a story of transition and how it shaped my opinion of what transition is or might be for women.

What Will You Learn?

Women and Transition: Reinventing Work and Life serves as a transition reference manual and a straightforward how-to guide for those interested in making a transition. The story is told in three sections: "Understanding Transition," "The Mechanics of Transitioning," and "Navigating Transition."

In "Understanding Transition," we define transition and explore the differences between change and transition. I introduce a framework for thinking about transition that is used throughout the book. We talk in detail about triggers, the events or feelings that typically initiate a transition cycle, and the emotions and feelings that accompany them. The section concludes with a discussion about the gendered nature of transition, acknowledging that both women and men have the potential to transition.

In "The Mechanics of Transitioning," I introduce readers to the two-stage transitioning process that I developed. It is a highly structured modular process that is customized to the needs of women in transition. We explore each step in detail and discuss how they fit together. The section also introduces readers to a readiness assessment designed to help readers decide whether or not they are ready for transition.

The final section, "Navigating Transition," is focused on helping readers begin. We discuss barriers we encounter in transition and some techniques to deal with them. We also review issues related to starting and lessons learned from those who have transitioned. The section concludes with a quick summary of the necessary items to pack as you prepare for the journey of transition.

What Impact Do I Hope to Have?

Writing this book has been nothing short of a labor of love. My guess is that you will sense this as you walk with me through its chapters. I hope that the information and tools provided help every woman reach her fullest potential, both personally and professionally. If successful, the book will inspire women to think carefully about the applicability of transition in their own lives. At a minimum it should raise the reader's awareness of transition and how best to approach it.

I hope that the book positions women as great decision-makers on their own behalf at the moment they face life events that could initiate transitions. I remember attending a speech by Alex D'Arbeloff, cofounder of Boston-based Teradyne, a multibillion-dollar semiconductor test equipment manufacturer. That day, he shared his goal in growing his outstanding company: to make sure every one of his employees was a great decision-maker. He reasoned that this skill would enable his company to succeed in innumerable ways. I think the same is true for women and transition. With education and awareness about transition, women can be fantastic decision-makers on their own behalf when faced with decisions related to transitions over the arc of their lives. Informed decisions at these moments can benefit not only ourselves and our families but also our society, whose continued growth and prosperity requires women's fullest engagement.

My biggest dream in writing this book is that it serves as a catalyst to bring fresh thinking to a host of topics that remain unresolved for women in our society. Without renewed debate, too many women will face insufficient policies and dated or discriminatory practices as they make decisions related to transition. Systemic issues like wage inequality or insufficient family leave practices or the lack of flexibility in our workplaces factor into decisions made by women in transition. By reframing these issues, my hope is that women can proceed with transitioning, while in parallel we work to make governmental, organizational, and social support structures more highly functional for all.

If we aggregate all women's experiences, the lens of transition also highlights the enormous talent leakage underway for women today in our society. Women are underemployed or unemployed in great numbers thanks to a host of issues—many addressable. Continuing to ignore these issues represents a significant long-term cost to our society.

If you take nothing else from the book, I hope you take away a belief in how valuable *your* questions are. How *you* see something and the questions *you* think to ask are invaluable in every situation in which you find yourself. This book all started because I asked a question: "how can I possibly reconcile my makeshift laundry room office with our society's characterization of women's progress?" Just a question. The more questions I asked, the more confident I got in the value that the answers held not just for me but for all women.

Thank You

I am eternally grateful to the women who agreed to talk with me about their transitions. These brave souls were pioneers because they participated long before I could offer conclusions or even a peek at any aggregate data. Thank you to each of you for your willingness to participate in the face of true uncertainty.

Each of the women's stories contained in the book is real and has been de-identified, meaning that no personally identifying information accompanies the stories. The majority of participants were college-educated women. They hailed from geographically and ethnically diverse backgrounds. Please join me in thanking them for their courage and honesty. Through their stories and mine I hope you will be able to calibrate your own experience with our collective one.

My greatest wish is that you enjoy this story of transition and its many surprises. I am grateful for the perspective that it has given me. It has offered me both grace and joy even as I have faced hardship and failure. Transition is a choice. It is not an easy one. Even so, I would struggle to characterize it as anything less than invaluable.

SECTION 1

Understanding Transition

CHAPTER 1

Change or Transition?

"She's fine," said my husband's voice on my cell phone as soon as the line engaged. *She* was our five-year-old kindergartner at the time. "What do you mean, she's fine?" I responded on the edge of panic.

When my phone rang I was stepping through the door to a trendy, gorgeously appointed restaurant on the banks of the Thames River in London, England. I was with 12 of my colleagues, a mixture of executives from our international and US businesses. Mostly they were men, save for me and one other woman.

We had been holed up in a conference room for the day discussing the international businesses' performance. Everyone seemed to enjoy the brief intake of fresh air on the quick walk between our offices and the restaurant. The Tower Bridge rose immediately in front of us.

I was at the rear of the group talking with a colleague, so it was easy to excuse myself to take the call. I slipped back out onto the sidewalk. It was a pavilion of sorts. Gray granite pavement stretched in every direction to accommodate pedestrian traffic along the river. The street seemed silenced by a long distance behind me. The Tower Bridge stood regally in front of me in the late afternoon light.

My husband went on to inform me that it was an early release day at my daughter's school. Early release, the bane of most working parents, is a day dedicated to teacher development during which children are let out of school earlier than regularly scheduled.

I was instantly happy that I had had the good sense to tell her teacher that I would be in London for the week. A simple step amid the swirl of reminders for Dad, the new nanny, two different schools, various neighbors, and Peapod, our local supermarket's delivery service. You get the picture?

Our five-year-old had stood waiting, with her Angelina Ballerina backpack, on the raised landing outside of the school's auditorium, an honorary zone reserved only for the school's kindergarteners at dismissal. Parents and care givers wait there for this daily ritual. That day no one arrived for my daughter.

After the rest of the class had been picked up, the teacher and his charge went to the office and called my husband. He in turn tagged our nanny who arrived with our younger son within ten minutes to get our daughter. All was well.

Or was it?

In that moment, standing in the shadows of the Tower Bridge, with a cell phone in my ear, I knew it. I was done.

That was it. An instant. This decision had not been the result of rigorous analysis or even casual daydreaming. It was a culmination of exhaustion, guilt, boredom, fear, and possibility.

I was done. But with what?

Less than a year later, my official transition would begin. At that moment on the Thames I had no understanding of what a transition was, let alone that I would go through one.

This chapter defines transition and traces the evolution of that definition in parallel with my own understanding of it. It also explores the difference between change and transition. The chapter delves more fully into one element of the definition of transition, identity. It concludes by positioning transition as a normal stage in adult growth and development, albeit one that is not widely understood.

A False Start

My official transition started in January 2010. At its outset I believed that this transition of mine was about reconciling the conflicts between my professional and personal lives. As I look back, however, I realize that the transition occurred for me in two stages: a false start that occurred five years before the afternoon on the Thames River, and a later, more authentic transition, a redefinition of my identity and my career, that followed an exhausting and stressful period for me and everyone around me. The false start sought to change something that I could control, a new job. I have learned that the false start did nothing more than amplify the underlying problems that it was intended to address. The real heartbreaker in it all was that this false start placed enormous stress on me and everyone around me, including my two preschool-aged children.

What was this false start? A job change that landed me in the C-suite of a Fortune 500 company. I had two children within 16 months of each other right around my fortieth birthday. I lost my dad five months after my youngest was born. At the time, I was working for a Texas-based company that had acquired the technology start-up that I had founded and led. Overnight I went from being an entrepreneur to a parent working in a large corporation. I was struggling to understand how to contribute in that environment while shuttling back and forth between Boston and Dallas on American Airlines. At the time, my husband was embarking on a new entrepreneurial venture, an exciting path on which he had deferred action for almost a decade. For both of us, larger questions like *"What's next for our new family?"* or *"What's next for Linda?"* never took precedence over a night of uninterrupted sleep.

My reaction at the time was "I need a new job." My priority? Eliminate spontaneous travel. Not all travel, mind you. Just the trips that required my presence at a meeting halfway across the country on 24 hours' notice. Like any sleep-deprived adult, I hastily made a list of the other things that I also needed. I loved emerging businesses. I wanted to work with someone who knew me. I really wanted a role with profit and loss responsibility, or at the very least a role with customer relationship responsibilities. It had not occurred to me how very unrealistic this was becoming.

Networking brought me to an opportunity with a former colleague who worked for Iron Mountain, a Fortune 500 company whose headquarters were located eight miles from my house. If I took the job, it would not require an airline flight between Boston and Dallas to simply attend my boss's staff meeting. Though it did not meet all of the criteria that I had set out for myself, I accepted a role as Executive Vice President of HR and Administration for a 21,000-person company, never having worked before in a staff function let alone human resources. In a traditional corporation, staff functions, like information technology, finance, or human resources, are typically support roles that enable other customer-facing functions. Ever the entrepreneur with a high comfort level with ambiguity, off I went.

Many wonder how I could have possibly gotten that job given that my background was in technology. The colleague referenced above, with whom I networked, felt confident in my skill set based upon our prior work together. He had served on the advisory board of the technology start-up that I led. In that capacity we had worked together on many strategic issues. For example, he played an advisory role to me as I negotiated the sale of the business. His company was subsequently acquired by Iron Mountain, a transaction that immediately put him in an executive leadership role. He wanted a business person to partner with him to run HR and to help him transform the company. It would be less travel, or so we discussed during my candidacy. Problem solved.

Change versus Transition

Although I was unaware of it, my decision to join Iron Mountain was a well-executed *change*. I did not have the bandwidth at the time to do more than address what I saw as the biggest challenge: I needed a new job with little travel. My focus on travel distracted me away from the underlying causes that were driving the need for that change. Instead, the underlying drivers would emerge five years later following my afternoon on the Thames.

Let us be clear. Change is not the same thing as transition. William Bridges, who authored the classic *Transitions: Making Sense of Life's Changes*,[1] made the most cogent argument I have read about the difference between change and transition. In the book he argued that "changes are driven to reach a goal, but transitions start with letting go of what no longer fits or is adequate to the life stage you are in."[2] Bridges, writing for a nongendered audience, noted that many of us "use change to avoid transition."[3] For Bridges, transition can be confused with change or deferred by change. In hindsight, this classification made enormous sense to me.

Bridges introduced a simple three-stage process for transition in his book. His construct started with "an ending," followed by an "empty zone," or "neutrality," followed by a "beginning."[4] Endings, in Bridges's experience, while necessary and healthy parts of transition, are bits of life that we typically are not great at. In this earliest stage of transition, Bridges said we "break our connection with the setting in which we've come to know ourselves."[5]

The process that he described was not for the faint at heart. He characterized endings as difficult. However, he was also quick to note that transition led to revised purpose, energy, and renewal for those willing to proceed through the earliest—and hardest—stages.

Other scholars made similar arguments to Bridges's view of the fundamental nature of transition. Robert Kegan, a decade after Bridges's *Transitions*, defined a similar progression in *The Evolving Self*.[6] He concluded that "all growth is costly. It involves the leaving behind of an old way of being in the world. Often it involves, at least for a time, leaving behind the others who have been identified with that old way of being."[7] Kegan focused on *adaptation* as a central organizing theme of one's life experience over time. Similar to Bridges's endings, Kegan's adaptation was associated early on with differentiating or separating from one's former self. Later the process was characterized by a re-engagement or integration phase, which was described using adjectives like attachment and inclusion, with a newer version of one's self.

As I joined Iron Mountain, I was unaware of the work of both authors. I did, however, believe that I was off on a new beginning. I fully believed that my problems were solved. Case closed. My beginning, however, was inconsistent with the definition of *beginning* in transition as defined by both Bridges and Kegan.

An Early Definition of Transition

As I started my new job, it was easy to redirect the adrenaline that I had once survived on within a technology start-up toward my new C-suite life. The topics that we took on were engaging, strategic, and impactful. We worried about how our employees might fare if the growth rate of our main business slowed or turned negative. We explored what we would need to be successful if we entered new businesses or new international markets. Employees stood at the heart of these issues. Early on, it was easy to engage intellectually, while I placed my other more personal demands, like the needs of my family, on autopilot.

As the honeymoon period wore off, though, I realized that I had landed myself another extreme job, albeit one with more predictable but no less travel. I had added another element too, a steep learning curve, thanks to my prior career outside of the HR arena. Sylvia Ann Hewlett coined the phrase "extreme job" in her 2007 book *Off-Ramps and On-Ramps: Keeping Talented Women on the Road to Success*.[8] Hewlett's definition of an extreme job is one that requires 60 hours or more per week, is well paid, and has additional characteristics like requiring work-related events outside of regular hours, large amounts of travel, large numbers of direct reports, or always-on client availability 24/7.[9] That last characteristic affects nearly every knowledge worker I know in today's technology-infused hyperconnected society. Would all knowledge worker jobs now be defined as extreme?

In spite of the job's extreme demands, I worked very well with my boss, the CEO, a forward-looking leader. At the time, I appreciated what I perceived as the flexibility his leadership style afforded me. His favorite saying was, "You can work any 60 hours you want." Two in the morning. Eleven at night. *You choose.* The only element of the environment that concerned me was that I was the only person in the C-suite and on the 12-member leadership team with a working spouse. Yes, I was the only female. I expected that. But the lack of other working spouses really bothered me.

The tricky part of this false start was that I loved my work and the people with whom I got to engage. I was not put off by the demands of the job. It only worked, however, because I had Mary Poppins as a nanny. *Nanny* is really an insufficient term to describe her. She was an incredible professional with a diverse skill set. She took care of all of us. This level of partnership and professionalism is available to very few, thanks in no small part to the outsized earnings capabilities of jobs like the one I had. I truly believe that without this incredible woman, the "false" nature of my job change to Iron Mountain would have revealed itself to me years earlier. Why? Things would have unwound sooner.

Mary Poppins left us about six months prior to my afternoon on the Thames River. Her departure would mark another milestone in my evolution toward an official transition.

My starting definition of transition was *a process I needed to go through to reconcile the demands of my personal life with those of my professional life.* I expected that this process would lead me to a new job, albeit a unique one. Maybe no travel. Maybe less than full time. I was not sure. I was only certain that I could not replicate the job I had just left because the scope and intensity were taking a huge toll on me physically and emotionally. I was thoroughly exhausted, having survived on five hours of sleep a night for years. I could not proceed in that frame anymore.

Initial Benchmarks

Early on I sensed that this starting definition might be not quite right. Immediately upon leaving my job I began to explore new opportunities that would reconcile my two competing realities. I also started to listen to the voices of other women who found themselves in similar situations although for different reasons. Some early observations and conversations with these women led me to think that a change in direction was much more complicated than what I had initially thought. Two women's stories really opened my eyes to this.

Sarah was a hard-charging type-A individual. I met her at a coffee shop in suburban DC after a friend introduced us. She clutched an iPhone in one hand and a Starbuck's coffee cup in the other. She was focused and intense. In speaking with her I began to understand that the cell phone embrace was optimistic. She would talk for a minute or two and then swipe the screen on her phone to awaken it. She was hoping to see an inbound message from a potential new employer with whom she had recently interviewed. The company had committed to getting back to her by the end of the week. It was Friday morning.

Sarah was looking for a job. She had three children, two in middle school and one in high school. Most days she juggled the demands of family life: aspiring basketball players, a budding science geek, the occasional community service project, and an affable cat that loved to swallow small objects. She described a household in a constant state of mild commotion.

Sarah seemed both gifted and fair minded. If I had met her in the workplace, I am sure that I would have been impressed with her ability and work ethic. You could tell that she had a no-nonsense approach. Her background had been in medical device sales. She had a track record of success, and was used to the financial rewards that accompanied it.

"My transition has ebbed and flowed over the past decade," she shared. "I wasn't aware of the need for it until well into a surprisingly difficult process which took a huge personal toll."

"For a minute, I kind of felt lucky," she explained. "I was expecting my third child. The company that I worked for was going through a reorganization. Just before I was about to go out on maternity leave, my boss told

me I could take a buy-out package. Eighteen months full salary. Benefits."
She described feeling as if she had won the lottery.

"I never considered not working. But this was like an incredible offer."
Sarah went on to describe the package's rich benefits, whose financial
value would far exceed the 12-week maternity leave that she planned to
cobble together from short-term disability and vacation pay.

In hindsight she scoffed a bit at her naiveté. She reasoned incorrectly
that she could just go get another job after the time she planned to take
off for her maternity leave. When she started to look for work, she initially
tried to secure part-time work. "Part time doesn't exist," she fumed in
retelling her story. "Don't believe what you read in the papers." She was
tipped off to this reality right out of the gate. Her prior employer, whom
she approached first, was flummoxed by her request for part time. Their
response? How could her role possibly be done *part time*? After concluding
that part time was not realistic, Sarah sought full-time work. Yet despite
herculean efforts, she remained out of the workforce for most of the next
five years.

Sarah described herself during this time as very disconnected and
ungrounded. "The financial pressures are overwhelming," she said. The
impact on her went well beyond financial. The transition had enacted a
significant emotional toll that she had been unprepared for. She struggled
with her loss of identity. Her self-confidence eroded. She said, "I've low-
ered my expectations for a job and for income. Honestly, I don't know that
I would ever have stopped working. I should not have stopped. During
this period that unexpectedly lasted five years, I felt that I could disappear
and nobody would notice."

In listening to Sarah tell her story, I began to hear an undercurrent of
something far more complex than finding a flexible employer. Her statements stretched beyond the balance of personal and professional demands.
I started to question whether my beginning definition of "transition" as
the process of reconciling these two demands was much too narrow.

Katy's story was the other one that blew my sense that a job change
would be the easy and correct path. Katy was a dynamic single woman
who found herself in retirement sooner than she had ever planned. She
lived in Los Angeles County, where she served as a divisional CFO for a
large publicly traded holding company. Her career in finance had been

spent in a series of progressively larger and larger divisions of that same corporation. Her roles and level of success demanded punishing 6 a.m. to 8 p.m. days. She noted, "I had achieved my goals. I didn't have any unfinished career goals."

She had seriously considered resigning for almost a year prior to retiring. Her retirement was precipitated by the company's substantial reorganization, which was something she did not expect but that ultimately played to her favor.

"As soon as I left, the importance of *large corporate* fell away," she said. She described her state of mind immediately following the retirement as "exhausted" and "scary." I could certainly relate to her description of exhaustion.

She found the transition hard and humbling. She was too young to retire and wanted a long-term financial plan. After she spent some time reflecting on what might come next, she realized that she liked the control she now had in her life as opposed to working for a large company that dictated her choices. "I am more intertwined with who I am. I am less about someone else's standard, like the corporation's, than my own standard. I finally gave myself the freedom," she said. Katy found part-time work through a social ventures group she joined early in her transition. She was surprised by how meaningful she found her new work. She loved her transition and the life she unexpectedly defined as a result of it.

While Sarah's story revealed to me that my definition of "transition" was too narrow in scope, Katy's story began to show me that it was too superficial. Transition was far richer than a change in jobs or the decision to retire. Transition involved reordering priorities, letting go of those that no longer fit, and, as Katy's story seemed to suggest, finding one's voice. Early on, I thought transition was a process that I could step through relatively quickly. After all, I had had a few jobs, and I had worked in fast-paced, high-powered situations, so why could I not get the job I sought relatively quickly? This conclusion was more and more unrealistic or, maybe in line with Sarah's experience, somewhat naive.

Immediately after I left Iron Mountain, I filled my time...networking...consulting...volunteering. I got a political appointment to a civic board in my town. I chaired a special Science, Technology, Engineering and Math (STEM) event at my children's school. I called a cousin on her birthday for the first time in almost 20 years. She was speechless and instantly concerned for my well-being. Can you see the pattern? I replaced the craziness of my former life with an equally busy, albeit local, reality.

Even though my initial definition of transition was insufficient, I was still not able to articulate why. I still had the belief that something more was possible for me. This growing feeling was highlighted by my reaction to job opportunities that came my way during my retreat to a busy, locally defined reality. None of the job opportunities held my attention even though they each had attractive features. There needed to be more. I knew I needed to trust that instinct. At that time, however, it was not obvious how I would do so.

The Definition of Transition Broadens

Over time I realized that I was just filling time, and in fact I was completely unable to process how to be silent on a random Tuesday morning. Or said better, I began to realize that my biggest fears were rooted in the silence that accompanied an empty schedule. I had spent a quarter century working six days a week, happiest in a scrum of people and ideas. I was one of those people who loved to work. It was my hobby. My passion.

Thanks to my growing awareness of this fear, I came to believe that the silence was necessary in advancing my thinking about what transition really meant. In parallel I continued to listen to the voices of other women who had progressed through the earliest stages of transition prior to me. Two other stories convinced me that I might need to think differently.

"I do outsourced market research for small companies," shared Tracy. We were having tea in a small coffee shop on McKinney Avenue in Dallas. "For the first 20 adult years of my life, I would have never thought I could run a business. I didn't think I had the knowledge to do it. The courage to do it. People wouldn't pay me for what I did."

Tracy became an entrepreneur in a roundabout way via complex and emotionally draining fertility issues. She and her husband were adopting a child soon, her first of three adopted children, and she wanted to be around her new baby as much as possible. She said of entrepreneurship, "'I'll just try this' because I knew that I was having my son, and the first four months the adoption agency wants you to be with her.

"It was a big shift in thinking. I remember being excited and scared to death." That day in a nearly deserted coffee shop, Tracy offered me a glimpse of the emotional turmoil that led to her starting her own business. She lost twins late in her first pregnancy. She talked of the horrific experience of returning to work without the twins in her life following a near full-term pregnancy. "No one knows what to say." She and I both fought back tears as she told that story.

A year after that experience she began a cycle of devastating miscarriages. She described a period of close to five years during which fertility issues became a constant focus for her and her husband. It was a roller coaster of emotions over a repetitive pattern of events. The ups and downs, the medications, the crushing losses. It was all too much. One day she said, "Enough. We're adopting." She described her decision as a slowly evolving conclusion. It required her to reorient her sense of self and of her future. It was a radical shift.

I could not help but compare Tracy's and Katy's and Sarah's experiences with my own. We were all experiencing lack of alignment in our lives, whether it was due to work-family conflict, or being ready for a new chapter in life, or thanks to a mismatch between our needs and the environment within which we were used to participating. It was not just child care or the demands of a family at play, because Katy faced similar issues as a single adult woman. It was not particulars about workplace demands, because these women participated in vastly different work environments. Medical equipment. Market research. Finance. Sales. What else was going on?

Elizabeth was a thoughtful and strong woman who in her late twenties had been a PhD candidate at UCLA on a full scholarship. She chuckled a bit as she retold the story about the idealistic vision of academia that she held back then. Once inside the hallowed halls, however, her eyes were opened by some traumatic events. One involved senior faculty members who misused the work of doctoral candidates. These same faculty members would later sit in judgment of the candidates' dissertations. Highly principled Elizabeth struggled with the pervasiveness of this issue. It did not take much more to convince her that academia was inconsistent with "who I wanted to be."

"It was a time of great pain," she shared. "Up until that time my package was defined. I thought that my attractiveness to other people was about my being smart." Despite her own clarity about not becoming a professor, she found that leaving academia was incredibly destabilizing. She joked that everyone always knew her as "someone who was smart, someone who was academic." Without that anchor, who would she be? It seemed to me that Elizabeth took the notion of transition further than the other three. She knew at the outset that the answer to her problem was not just leaving academia. It was a "radical renovation" of herself.

In talking with each of these women I began to understand that most were experiencing something more comprehensive than a simple reconciliation of competing demands in their lives. As I was executing my own job search, I had a growing realization that the same was true for me. The next step would require something more significant than just getting a new job.

A Revised Definition

It was this initial realization that led me to another definition for transition. Transition is a process that requires us to *reimagine our notion of self*. I was captivated by this idea. By this revised definition, it seemed that every woman I met was experiencing transition on some level. But no one knew how to talk about it. Popularly or culturally accessible vocabulary for an evolution at this level just did not exist.

At this time I began experimenting with the topic of women's transition in a more structured way by starting a blog, Novofemina.com, an exploration of women's transition. I realized that I was sharing data from an extremely limited sample, my own. So I had to be careful with the kinds of insights I could share. But my curiosity fueled this endeavor, and I decided to seek out more stories, that is, samples from women who would be willing to share their experiences. Without really even trying, I had over 100 women and a few men participate in a survey that I pulled together.

The survey relied on this broader definition of transition, "reimagining our notion of self." Respondents were all college educated or higher. One third had no children. To my surprise, more than 80 percent of respondents were either in transition or had transitioned within the past five years. Those 45 and under had a slightly higher likelihood of transition, 88 percent. While 79 percent of those over 45 had done so.[10] As these respondents looked forward, a staggering 92 percent stated that they expected to transition again in the future.

The survey asked women to share the specifics of their transitions, why they needed to transition, and the barriers they faced. It was an initial rich introduction to the breadth of issues women face under the umbrella of transition. Barriers cited were related to financial pressures, access to jobs or opportunities, and limitations in the ability of a woman's network to help her navigate to new opportunities. Most respondents cited a mismatch between their need for flexibility and the flexible arrangements available to them from a wide range of employers.

The survey helped me refine a growing set of hypotheses that I had about women and transition.

- Transition for women occurred over the arc of their lives. It did not seem driven by age or the presence or absence of certain aged-related events, like childbirth.
- Transition occurred repeatedly for women over the course of their lives. Sixty-seven percent of respondents alluded to having transitioned more than three times.
- It seemed that both intentional and unintentional triggers could initiate transition. These included change in health status, divorce, childbirth, loss of a job, marriage and retirement, as well as the decision to pursue more of one's potential. In fact this last trigger was one of the single highest triggers cited in the survey.
- Transitions, regardless of the trigger, shared many common characteristics.

Women who completed the survey had the ability to provide stories of their transitions in an open-ended way. Their responses offered me a glimpse into a rich and complex world. Two themes emerged quickly from this qualitative data. First, capacity, or a woman's belief in what might be possible for her, was expressed as a factor consistently and in countless ways. Many spoke about capacity in their stories of entrepreneurial or nontraditional work opportunities—decisions that often emerged in response to barriers that impeded their original course. Still others noted their surprise when citing capacity in that they succeeded far beyond their known comfort zones. For example Jeanie, a mid-fifties woman who had never worked outside the home, shared that she was thrilled to start a home-care not-for-profit in the aftermath of the death of her spouse for whom she had cared throughout his long illness.

The other theme that emerged from the qualitative data was a strong preference among women for work that held meaning or was in alignment with their personal values. Hewlett offered a perspective on this in her *Off-Ramps and On-Ramps: Keeping Talented Women on the Road to Success*.[11] Hewlett said, "Women seek meaning and connection in their work lives."[12] Many respondents to the survey had initiated job changes because of misalignment over values expressed in their workplaces.

The survey bolstered my belief that transition needed to address substantive themes that were specific to women as they navigated the recurring topic of transition in their lives.

Following the administration of the survey, I was speaking to a friend about a painful period in her life. Karen, a classmate of mine from the Harvard Business School, always beams as she describes her two beautiful daughters, one about to graduate from college and the other still working her way through. Her joyfulness is amplified by an exhale. Finally, an exhale. For Karen, this plateau was hard won following a decade that included a painful, long-drawn-out divorce. She is a gifted operations executive who works in a closely held, privately owned company. She started there because she needed a job, not because it was her passion. That she reserves for her daughters.

She described the moment when she knew her divorce was inevitable: "I felt my entire being was squelched by that relationship." Even though she was resolute in her decision to leave the marriage, she described the period as a complete shift in her values because she never wanted to be divorced. "I never wanted to go down that path. It was letting go of everything I grew up with as far as the values and what divorce and marriage meant." Two things Karen said really struck me: "letting go" and "values." In light of the initial survey data, I began to hear more of these linkages between values and choices. The survey respondents, a self-selected group of well-educated adults, frequently referenced professional choices that were influenced by values. It seemed like a departure from the life-long linear—largely male-defined—career models that I had embraced up until that point. It did align with my understanding of the linkages that millennials made in their workplace choices, particularly those that

I experienced as an HR executive. I remember that a dear friend took me to lunch about a year into my transition. She was surprised and curious, "Why did you stop?" she asked, referencing the fact that I was not working full time. "You of all people." If I chose to continue to explore transition, my departure from the prior path would be stark.

A Catalyst

About one year into my official transition, a friend called to tell me that she had gotten a new job. She had been laid off from her former employer, only to land a job within a few weeks. The new job seemed like a great opportunity. She was thrilled with the prospect of how it all worked out because she was facing college tuition for her high school-aged children. She would be able to put her unexpected severance package toward college tuition. The new job offered a higher salary and more responsibility. The universe seemed to be smiling.

When I hung up the phone, I could not help but do a comparison between the time she had been out of work and the time I had been out of work. In the year since I had been in transition, I had worked on part-time consulting gigs and created my busy—some days frenetic—local existence. Her call catapulted me into an irrational comparison between our two experiences that was heavily influenced by society's expectations. My transition was marked by lots of these moments of critical self-judgment. Some of my favorite admonishments were, *"Why can't I just get a job that fits my requirements?"* Or *"Maybe I will never work again."* Even when I escaped these irrational thoughts, I wondered, *"Why am I opting out during the highest earning years of my career?"*

I kept toggling between my own reaction to my situation and my friend's great news. I reached out to a professional colleague, Ralph Roberto, President, Keystone Partners, a career management and leadership development firm in Boston. He offered an interesting perspective. When experiencing a job loss he said, "People don't often see a *gain* to staying out of the full-time workforce. Some people don't have any desire to look beyond replicating a job that they just had. They enjoy it. It fits their lifestyle." Roberto's perspective helped clarify the differences between change and transition. My friend's objective in searching for a new job was similar to my own when I joined Iron Mountain. I sought a change targeted at specific issues. Similar to her, I was successful in addressing those that I prioritized.

But years later I found myself asking bigger questions about what I really wanted from my work and the impact I hoped to have. Prior to that point, my identity had been largely defined in a narrow image of lifelong linear workplace progression. While I had thrived in that environment for decades, I knew that was not what I wanted in my next move. I knew that the meaning and values present in the work were just as important as the company's brand, the compensation, and the status of a well-regarded title.

Despite this growing understanding, I still had days when my prevailing internal voice was far from cheerful. I joked with friends that the negative emotions of transition—fear, shame, guilt, and uncertainty, to name a few—were visited upon me Scrooge-esque depending upon the day. Even with all of those emotions, I was becoming aware that I could not survive by jumping back into a job that was someone else's view of what was right for me.

The Final Definition for Transition

I concluded that my "notion of self" definition for transition was also incomplete. I finally understood Bridges's distinction between change and transition by comparing my beliefs at my transition's outset with my beliefs after listening to these women. It was becoming apparent that transition was less event driven and more process driven. It seemed to involve choice. An informed choice. I decided on the following definition: transition requires a choice, one that we make when faced with the need to change. We can choose to change or to transition. Not everyone chooses transition. Many people, including me prior to joining Iron Mountain, choose *change*, believing wholeheartedly that it is in fact what was is needed at the time. Many succeed there. For those who decide to pursue more than a new change, transition requires an informed decision to act. *Transition is a process that requires us to re-examine our assumptions about identity, capacity, and values.* It is multistep and iterative. We envision. We test. We learn. We integrate our learnings. We refine our initial thoughts. We test again. We grow.

At last I was sure I had something more concrete with which to work.

The Role of Identity in Women's Transition

Identity played a substantive role in my revised definition of transition. Many women with whom I spoke referenced identity in some fashion. In fact, several women who discussed this idea with me thought that *capacity* and *values* felt redundant to the use of identity. Were they not both a part of identity? Identity's cameo role in the transition definition led me to investigate identity further.

Patrice, a woman who served as an executive in a large telecommunication organization, offered a unique perspective on identity. She had just retired, but did not believe that she wanted to fully disengage from the workforce. She sought postretirement employment, but was not sure if what she was seeking was a job or a new career. Together we laughed because we were not sure what to call it.

She was no stranger to transition, because earlier in her career she had moved from a teaching role into a corporate research role, a move plagued by financial and career uncertainty. As she sought her postretirement work, she said, "So this really is *my* problem. I can figure out what I want to do, I can be anything I want to be. It's also confusing. I can be anything I want to be. It's like being a teenager again. You know, when they ask you what do you want to be when you grow up? Well, who knows?" Her voice rose several octaves on those last words. She went on to add, "My dear husband and all of my friends don't quite get it." She continued, "You know, they love me and so they sort of try to be there for me. But it is just so incredibly difficult. They seem to be saying to me, 'If that's how you've always identified yourself, and you don't identify yourself that way anymore, then who are you?'" She was struggling with how to define herself at the very same time that her immediate social network was reacting to her process and its meaning in their own lives.

Psychologists, social scientists, and philosophers for centuries have debated the definition of identity. One definition I found useful was presented by Nancy P. Rothbard and Lakshmi Ramarajan in "Checking Your Identities at the Door? Positive Relationships between Nonwork and Work Identities."[13] They say, "Identity relies on a set of subjective knowledge that is considered to mean, *I am*."[14] People can define themselves as members of groups, as partners in close relationships, and in terms of personal aspects or traits. "Because identities are a type of knowledge (knowledge about oneself) identites can be activated,"[15] turned on or off. "Individuals often hold up to five to seven important identities although they may be at various stages of activation at any one time."[16]

I chose to adopt a simple definition of identity for our purposes: *how we make meaning in our lives.* There are countless factors that can influence identity formation, everything from families and communities and education to the experiences we have in our lives, like success or failure. When faced with the need to change, a person has a choice. Ideally it is an informed choice. The choice to re-examine does not mean you will adopt something "new." It simply requires one to engage in the act of reimagining, examining.

Historical Perspective on Women's Identity

I am not the first to explore the concept of identity as it relates to women. Anna Fels, psychiatrist and author of the 2004 *Necessary Dreams: Ambition in Women's Changing Lives,*[17] said, "Women in the midst of their adult lives, not men, are faced with continuous pressure to re-evaluate and reshape their lives—a process by which women create, realize, reconfigure and abandon goals."[18] Betty Friedan, author of the seminal *The Feminine Mystique,*[19] held identity at the core of her thesis a half century ago. In the book, Friedan concluded that there was widespread unhappiness among women at the time. She reached her conclusions based on research conducted in the 1950s and 1960s. She argued that women's unhappiness was largely caused by their lack of identity outside of roles determined by biology or anatomy. She was also hypercritical of the media. The *feminine mystique,* in her mind, was a false notion created largely by the media that women could be fulfilled simply (or only) through roles like housewife or mother. From Friedan's perspective the media at the time espoused that fulfillment could be gained via ownership of canary yellow consumer durables and other hollow concepts.

Said Friedan, "I think that this has been the unknown heart of the women's problem in America for a long time, this lack of private image. Public images that defy reason and have very little to do with women themselves have had the power to shape too much of their lives. These images would not have such power, if women were not suffering from a crisis of identity."[20]

Friedan was onto the importance of identity for women. Nearly every woman who participated in my survey referenced identity in some fashion. How many choose transition over change I wondered? Let us face it. We encounter countless situations throughout life that require us to evaluate, accept, or pursue change. I was curious about how many people actually went a step further and went beyond realizing the importance of identity to make an actual transition.

Is Transition Commonplace?

Understanding transition and the role that identity plays within it caused me to wonder what is the likelihood that a person will re-examine their identity? Robert Kegan, and Lisa Laskow Lahey, authors of *Immunity to Change*,[21] brought forward conclusions about identity and the prevalence of it changing over the course of someone's life.

Kegan and Laskow Lahey's research introduced transition as a normal stage of adult development, a developmental milestone akin to those through which children progress. In young children we carefully watch for signs of developmental milestones like gross motor skills, cognition, and social development. In fact, today's parents, grandparents, and other supportive adults watch carefully over young children, ever mindful that developmental delays are best addressed through early interventions. Kegan and Laskow Lahey established that similar milestones exist for adults.

Kegan and Laskow Lahey's conclusions positioned transition as a normal step in a process of growth and development for adults. Earlier thinking believed that adult emotional and psychological development reached its peak at the same time as physical development. That meant that by the time we stopped growing, in height, so too did our developmental capabilities reach their climax. This thinking embraced a concept of identity that would become largely immobile shortly after teenage growth spurts.

Kegan and Laskow Lahey identified three stages of adult development (see Figures 1.1 and 1.2). Each stage represents an opportunity for a new way to "make meaning" in one's life. Their research revealed that adults can ascend these stages and plateau over the course of their lives well beyond the time of entering their twenties. Every adult, female or male, has the opportunity to pursue such a progression.

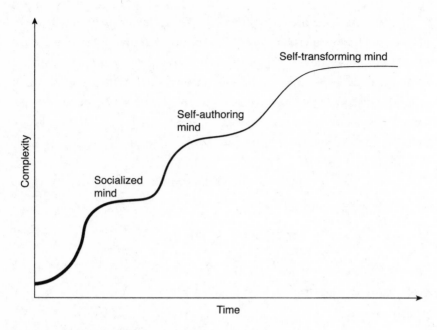

Figure 1.1 Three plateaus in adult mental development.
Source: Kegan and Laskow Lahey, *Immunity to Change,* 2009, 16.

The socialized mind
- We are shaped by the definitions and expectations of our personal environment.
- Our self coheres by its alignment with, and loyalty to, that with which it identifies.
- This can express itself primarily in our relationships with people, with "schools of thought" (our ideas or beliefs) or both.

The self-authoring mind
- We are able to step back from the social environment to generate an internal "seat of judgment" or personal authority that evaluates and makes choices about external expectations.
- Our self coheres by its alignment with its own belief system/ideology/personal code; by its ability to self-direct, take stands, set limits, and create and regulate its boundaries on behalf of its own voice.

The self-transforming mind
- We can step back from and reflect on the limits of our own ideology or personal authority; see that any one system or self-organization is in some way partial or incomplete; be friendlier toward contradiction and opposites; seek to hold on to multiple systems rather than projecting all but one onto the other.
- Our self coheres through its ability not to confuse internal consistency with wholeness or completeness, and through its alignment with the dialectic rather than either pole.

Figure 1.2 The three adult plateaus.
Source: Kegan and Lahey, 2009, p. 17.

The authors' conclusions offer a few provocative perspectives for transition. First, they argued that transition can occur at any point over the arc of our lives. At whatever age, transition constitutes the same psychological act, moving from one stage to the next which translates into modifications on how we make meaning in our own world. Thinking about this framework in terms of the women whom I was meeting, I could more easily understand the similarities in transition that I observed between a woman who was getting remarried and in the process welcoming three new children into her life, and another involved in the process of re-engagement in the workforce after she had launched three children. Was I correct in my observations?

Kegan and Laskow Lahey would say "maybe." Both women face different triggers to their transition: one a remarriage and expanded family, the other a career shift following the emergence out of an empty nest. Both women, when faced with a trigger, could proceed from a developmental construct like the socialized mind to the self-authoring mind. The data in Figure 1.2 tell us that the socialized mind relies entirely on alignment with and loyalty to that with which it identifies. The self-authoring mind relies upon its alignment with its own belief system or personal code, by its ability to self-direct, take stands, set limits, and create and regulate its boundaries on behalf of its own voice. For example, the woman getting remarried who demonstrates characteristics of the socialized mind might struggle with integrating her new family if her identity is rooted in expectations about what it means to be a 1950s nuclear family. Similarly, the empty nester might struggle if her notion of identity is rooted entirely in expectations of linear career progression. Re-engagement in the workforce or remarriage simply trigger a process of examination. The process is highly personal. The choice is up to each of the two women.

Kegan and Laskow Lahey also concluded that there is no dependent relationship between age and the developmental stages. Said another way, a 40-year-old woman who leads the care of a developmentally challenged child could exhibit the developmental capabilities of a self-authoring mind, whereas her next door neighbor, a 40-year-old female CFO, could exhibit the development capabilities of a socialized mind, the earlier developmental stage. Despite their same age, their developmental stages may differ.

Think about a woman who worked in a career defined by decades of upward linear progression and who upon retirement struggles if her identity is strongly aligned with the socialized mind stage. Her identity outside of her corporate persona may be adrift because she is no longer ensconced in the environment from which she derived meaning. Alternatively a postretirement woman with a self-authoring mind might be better able to articulate a series of self-directed postretirement work opportunities. Kegan and Laskow Lahey's conclusion supports my long-held belief that transition at retirement looks, acts, and feels no different from transition triggered by a remarriage at 48 years old. Both hearken to our identity and its potential mobility as we look forward.

How common is this shift? Do data exist about the frequency with which women, or men for that matter, proceed through these developmental stages? Some data and initial insights are available. Kegan and Laskow Lahey drew upon data from approximately 20 years ago to conclude that the majority of college-educated adults never fully achieve the plateau of the second stage of development, the self-authoring stage. Fifty-nine percent of college-educated adults in their survey achieved only the ascent to the second stage, the self-authoring stage.[22] Said another way, the majority of college-educated adults who participated in the research never fully transitioned beyond their initial identity. Many made progress in that direction, but few hit that next plateau. Less than 10 percent proceeded to the level of the self-transforming mind.[23]

Today's women are faced with a more complex set of roles than those typically ascribed to women even a generation ago. We hold descriptors like single heads of households, primary wage earners, multigenerational care providers, 24–7 workplace contributors, or working parents. Could these more complex roles affect the frequency with which women transition? Are women more than men forced to transition more frequently due to conflicts with our identity and the different roles we play in society? Has our identity's shelf life changed due to the complex realities of our modern lives? As we explore transition more fully, particularly whether or not it is gendered, we will come back to these types of questions.

Transition or Change

Transition started for me as a belief that something more was possible when I faced the need to change. At the time, I could not answer the question "what do you want to do?" My initial reaction to the uncertainty was to create a locally based, fast-paced reality that comfortably replicated my pretransition world. Surprisingly, none of the changes that I put forth at that time felt right. So I decided to explore transition in a fundamental way. I learned that changes were set forth to reach a specific goal, whereas transitions were something more.

Transition is a process that requires us to re-examine our assumptions about identity, capacity, and values. It requires a choice, an informed choice. Transition is a normal stage of adult growth and development— although one that is not widely understood nor discussed. Transition can occur in either gender and at any age.

Transition captivated my attention and gave voice to a meaningful, albeit unplanned, process that was unfolding in my life. That process— whose value was only becoming known to me as I defined transition— had only just begun.

CHAPTER 2

A Simple Framework

With the definition of transition in hand, I talked about it every chance I got. I quickly learned that, even though it engaged my listeners, more structure was required.

I was surprised by how often I encountered a single question: "Transition. How interesting. What type?" I got it everywhere I went. I wondered in listening whether the transitions themselves differed or whether there was something else at play. Gretchen, a candidate for an environmental engineering PhD, shared a story of her transition that differed from others I had heard. She arrived in Atlanta without a job after her partner got relocated. She cited the geographical move as a trigger for her transition. There was more at play than just a geographical move. "I didn't pay attention to the signals I was sending myself," she said of herself over the years leading up to the move to Atlanta. "The move was a late event in a long, evolving gradual transition process. There were ups and downs. My identity was wound up in being an environmental engineer. I ignored feelings that I wasn't happy on that path. There were signals. I didn't trust my own signals." The move forced Gretchen to listen more carefully to her instincts and begin a process of rethinking her assumptions.

What type of transition did Gretchen have? That question and the need for additional structure led me to create a framework, an anatomy for transition.

This chapter introduces a framework for transition, its anatomy. It explores the common characteristics of two of its elements: triggers and decisions. Later chapters discuss the final element of transition's anatomy, action.

Transition's Anatomy

Transition's anatomy is comprised of three parts: a trigger, a decision, and an action (see Figure 2.1). The anatomy's objective is to further one's understanding of the phases or stages involved in any transition process. The anatomy was designed using a construct similar to that used to understand stress.

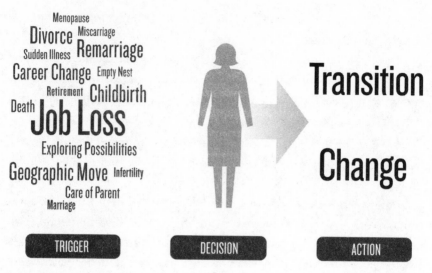

Figure 2.1 Transition's anatomy.

I learned about stress management by attending a weekend retreat at a local yoga center. A college friend of mine, Sydney, and I attended the session at Kripalu,[1] a yoga center housed in a former Jesuit monastery in western Massachusetts. Kripalu sits perched on a hill overlooking Tanglewood,[2] the summer home of the Boston Symphony Orchestra. The program we attended was held in an oversized room with cinder block walls very reminiscent of the building's Jesuit roots. Our instructor was patient and tried to create a stress-free environment in which to explore his topic. He introduced stress as a phenomenon comprised of two parts: stressors and stress. This classification allowed the instructor to present stressors separately from the experience of stress itself. He described how stressors were everywhere. A surly boss. A coworker. A family member. A mother-in-law. An illness. An upcoming presentation to the CEO. A non-communicative teenager. A spouse. A former spouse. Unemployment. A growing pile of bills. People, actions, or conditions. You name it. Stressors knew no boundaries. Each was valid. Real.

And stress? Simply the body's reaction to a stressor. Some people in attendance got anxious. Others overate. Still others lost sleep. One attendee had a significant life-altering response with the onslaught of chronic debilitating pain. All of these reactions—it was explained—were part of our body's defense mechanisms. Automatic. By isolating the components of stress, the instructor showed us how to advance our thinking about and our response to stress.

I borrowed the isolation technique from stress management and used it to look across many different women's transitions. With this lens I saw repetitive patterns. The lens also allowed me to isolate the events that initiated a transition process. Regardless of the trigger women described, I heard commonalities. Welcoming another baby. Changing careers. Menopause. Remarriage. An empty nest. Retirement. A sudden change in one's health status.

Continuing with what I learned at the stress seminar, I developed the idea that transition has a three-part anatomy: a triggering event, a decision point, and an action. A triggering event is the situation or thought that initiates a decision process. Once a triggering event occurs, a person has an opportunity to make a decision. The period of time between a triggering event and the actual decision can vary. The decision is the point at which an individual chooses to act in a certain direction. It is at this juncture that an individual can define the scope or breadth that she would like to pursue. Will she pursue change or transition?

The anatomy's final stage involves action, the process of transitioning itself. Transitioning is a multistep, iterative process that supports the re-examination of one's assumptions about identity, capacity, and values. It requires a fairly large commitment on the part of individuals who choose to undertake this process.

The anatomy purposely oversimplifies the complexity inherent in the decision step. In reality there are many decision options available to anyone at this juncture. For example, when faced with the need to change, you could choose the status quo, or defer change until a later date, or even choose a change that more accurately represents a turn back toward an earlier, more comfortable state. To change and to transition are by no means the only options available at that juncture. They are the two that we will focus on, however, in trying to increase our understanding of transition.

Part of the reason why I took the time to conduct the research and write this book was my own lack of understanding of this anatomy and its components. Prior to defining this structure, I was unable to parse out the triggering events that I experienced and their influence on the decisions that I made. As I mentioned earlier, I arrived at transition never having considered it. I approached the need for change in my life with a continually evolving list of goals targeted at addressing what I believed to be at play. I never even thought about the possibilities of change or transition after my children were born. I never considered that my identity might be at play, an identity almost entirely defined by my working persona. It was who I was. I loved it. And I fully believed that changing my job again would address the issues that I faced. I did not know how even to look at the complexity of the issues that were present and making me feel so unsettled. I thought it would work itself out, unassisted. Of course, it would take a fair amount of upheaval and real impact on those around me before I recognized this greater opportunity. My hope is that by my raising awareness about transition through this structure, other women will be able to adopt a path that is successful for them and far less circuitous than my own.

Understanding Transition's Triggers

A trigger, for our purposes, is a situation or thought that initiates a decision process. Marriage. Divorce. Childbirth. Menopause. Bereavement. Boredom. Sudden success. A geographic move. An empty nest. A career change. Death of a loved one. Exhaustion. Infertility. Job loss. Retirement. And countless more. In spite of our familiarity with all of these, triggers are multidimensional, nonlinear and can be accompanied by all manner of emotions.

Triggers do nothing more than represent an opportunity for a decision. Do the triggers in either of the following examples guarantee a transition? Rebecca was a director of Inside Sales at a large software and service organization in the Atlanta area. She was in her mid-fifties with grown children. "My trigger grew out of my relationship with my boss," she said. "A new executive team came into being at the company and my former boss was let go." Up until that point Rebecca had always had a great relationship with her boss. They had worked together for many years.

Over time they had developed their own pattern of working together. Rebecca described it in the following way: "I could say what I believed and felt, you know, inside of the office. But we always did what we needed to do to get it done." Maybe out of naiveté or her familiarity with this work style, she continued this pattern with her new boss.

"I slowly started to realize that I was being left out of meetings," she said. She was ultimately let go. "It was a relief when it finally happened," she added. Rebecca was sad and angry. The termination had been a huge blow to her confidence. To add to the humiliation she was experiencing, former colleagues kept calling her to say how surprised they were that she had been fired. She had given more than a decade to this company, and she had loved her job. It was a huge part of how she defined herself.

Rebecca identified the job loss as a trigger. It deposited her at the footsteps of a decision. How to proceed?

Janine was a product manager at a large West Coast-based specialty retailer. She started off by telling me that "there needs to be something more when I get to the office." You could tell from the way she began that she had been dealing with a lot of complexity inside and outside of her office. "I have three daughters. I was unexpectedly let go when my department was reorganized." Just 40, Janine described herself as very athletic, competitive. She played sports in high school and college.

"I went back and forth to Asia a lot. It was really a struggle going to work every day. With all the outsourcing that I have to do as a parent of young kids. The drop off. The nanny switches."

She described a growing void that she had felt in the environment where she worked. "There has to be something *more* when I get to where I'm going." This gap had been there a long time, probably since her children had been born. "I just never had the time to address it. Let's face it. With three kids, a 60-hour a week job, and going back and forth to Asia, when am I going to look for a job?"

Janine also identified the termination of her job as a trigger. But she also identified something more. She had a growing sense of disillusionment with the decisions she was watching senior management make. They were in conflict with her own values.

Janine and Rebecca each identified the same trigger, a job loss. Triggers are rarely single threaded, as evidenced by Janine's remarks. The triggers themselves do not guarantee an action. We give triggers agency, or meaning, in our lives.

My initial reaction to triggers was to bucket them in easily identifiable categories: voluntary or involuntary; visible or invisible; internal or external. But then I realized that it overcomplicated triggers to bucket them in this fashion. Both Rebecca and Janine experienced involuntary events, job losses, but this classification alone seemed insufficient to describe the thinking processes initiated by the triggering event. Remember Elizabeth's decision to withdraw from the PhD program, discussed in chapter 1? When I asked about her transition's trigger, she cited pain. "I wish I could say that my triggers were an awakening or a higher self-knowledge," she said of the many transitions that she had encountered in her life. "It's always been pain. And it would often take a fairly sharp degree of pain before I was willing to ask myself important questions." Elizabeth was one among many women who referenced meaningful questions about her identity, or who she wanted to be, as the most important trigger to her transition. This authentic trigger revealed itself to Elizabeth after a series of other triggers, like the misuse of her work by senior-level colleagues.

Triggers are multidimensional and seem to work in concert with each other to compel us toward action. One of the best examples of this was shared by Mary, a late forties retired US Army Lt. Colonel. She had held logistics and operational roles in the service, thanks to her advanced degrees in industrial and mechanical engineering. From the outside, people might conclude that Mary's transition was triggered by retirement. After all, she filed her paperwork after a more than 20-year career and retired from the service.

A closer exploration revealed something else entirely. Mary's triggers were personal and yet invisible. When asked to describe the events leading up to her retirement, she immediately shared that she was tired of moving every two years, a requirement for service members who want to continue to ascend the ranks of military service. She was also exhausted after years of 13–14 hour days. Even more disheartening was that the jobs available to her as she progressed up the ranks seemed less and less engaging. There was another dimension at play as well. The persistent loss. Too many of her military friends had lost their lives as a result of their service.

One day as Mary was readying herself for yet another geographic move, she woke up and said, "I'm done." There was no more analysis than that. She had come to the end of her line. As she looked back on the decision during our conversation, she thought that her real trigger stemmed from decades of having to relocate every two years. She knew she wanted to put roots down in a community. Full stop.

Once Mary initiated her transition, she explored ways to leverage her experience and achieve her desired objective. It took a series of iterative steps in order to do so. She quickly established herself in Seattle, thanks in no small part to a job opportunity with a military contractor. The job gave her two important gifts: a salary and a destination postretirement. While all this was positive, she was not so enamored with her initial work experience in her postretirement career. She favored the chain-of-command and clearly articulated decision-making infrastructure that she had come to know as a member of the military. More importantly, Mary experienced a deep sense of loss for the military community with which she had always been affiliated. It was not so much their vocabulary or physical presence that she missed. It had more to do with their approach to community, a community that seamlessly integrated military families and mobilized to take care of their needs in the broadest sense. Mary gave me one example: tire-changing brigades that sprang up to put snow tires on cars for families who had service members deployed overseas. She really desired to be a part of a community that looked at the needs of its members in an equally broad fashion. As Mary's transition progressed, she continued through a cycle of framing and reframing a new identity, a postmilitary version of herself. Even though she exited the military, components of her military identity, like active engagement in a community, infused how she defined herself.

Once in Seattle, Mary immersed herself in a not-for-profit dedicated to supporting families of breast cancer patients. The activity engaged her spirit and helped as she looked for full-time work following her resignation from the military contractor job.

Mary experienced voluntary visible triggers like retirement or dissonance with moving. She also experienced internal triggers like exhaustion and a desire to put down roots in a geographic community, one in which she could remain for more than two years. All of these triggers together challenged Mary to think through who she wanted to be.

While triggers were often multidimensional, they were not always negative. Theresa, a late forties administrator at a well-known West Coast technology company, shared her decision to take early retirement from her job where she had worked for more than 20 years. "I got this unbridled optimism at the beginning because I had made the choice to leave myself."

She described a richly engaging career, but one that *unfolded*, not one that she ever actively *chose*. Early in her career she had backed into the job. She had taken it as a temporary placeholder to fill in a gap in employment immediately following her former husband's relocation. Once inside the organization, she never initiated a job search again. She commented, "I had a series of jobs, and you keep getting more responsibility and your salary goes up and this and that happens. You know, you move up and get more responsibility and somehow you stay."

Just prior to her decision to retire, she encountered some behaviors on the part of senior management that were out of sync with the values that she believed in and that the organization had espoused as their own for many years. This disconnect served as a trigger for her to act on her own behalf. She described an excitement that bordered on euphoric in making the decision. "It was so empowering because I made the choice. I owned the choice." After her going along for many years, this trigger led to something that was positive and uplifting. Theresa's sense of herself changed. Her trigger was a disillusionment with the behaviors of senior leadership in the organization. It fueled a rethinking that led to action.

The experience of triggers is a nonlinear, highly individualized cycle. Gretchen, the environmental science PhD candidate from whom we heard earlier, described her triggers as occurring repeatedly over time and gaining in strength. Her early triggers occurred in small ways, which she described as "an instinct that something wasn't right." She did not choose to address them. Her partner's move to Atlanta was a more significant trigger. She finally resolved to consider the Atlanta move as an opportunity to think more completely about who she wanted to be.

I did not uncover a single "correct" pattern for triggers. Like Gretchen's, some women experienced cycles full of repetitive triggers. Others described a single trigger that led to a period of reflection, followed by a decision. Regardless of the pattern, triggers themselves served as a precursor to a decision.

Triggers are multidimensional, occur in a nonlinear pattern, and are accompanied by many thoughts and emotions. We give agency to triggers.

We assign – most often unknowingly – the thougths and feelings that accompany them. Chapter 3 explores in detail our reactions to transition, including the emotions and feelings that accompany its triggers.

A Decision

The second stage in transition's anatomy is a decision—making an informed choice to act. At its simplest, this stage requires a woman to consciously decide to initiate a re-examination of her assumptions about identity, capacity, and values. It involves answering the question "what should I do?" This question has presented itself countless times in all of our lives. In transition, it asks about our willingness to interrogate who we are and how we make meaning in our world. Are those concepts about yourself mutable or immutable? Similar to triggers, the action represented in the decision step seems to be nonlinear and individualized.

The decision to act manifests itself in many ways. It can range anywhere from the women who experience moments of instantaneous clarity to those whose decisions are intertwined with long periods of growing self-awareness.

Several women referenced a meaningful deepening in their self-awareness as a prerequisite to their decision. While that in fact may be a common denominator for some transitions, I was not able to isolate a growing self-awareness as a factor across the entire sample of those who shared their stories with me. I did, however, hear of a variety of "realizations" that occurred for women as their thinking about a possible transition matured. The realizations ranged from learnings like, "becoming clearer on what mattered to them" to realizing the power or usefulness of a strength that had been dormant. Susan Duffy, Executive Director of Babson College's Center for Women's Entrepreneurial Leadership,[3] shared an interesting perspective on realization and transition. She discussed with me the behaviors she witnessed in the cohort of female entrepreneurs with whom she works. Of transition she said, "It starts with a 'realization' that this is open to you. The realization begins when women understand that it is not just for a few lucky people." She described the phenomenon of women not only realizing that their dreams were possible but that they could define an avenue upon which to fulfill those dreams.

Other women cited the reconciliation of gating issues as an enabler to their decision. A gating issue is an issue that serves as a temporary blockage requiring resolution prior to advancing further. Phoebe, a very thoughtful women in her early forties, said, "I finally put my foot down about a decision not to have children. I can finally put this decision on the shelf and focus on other decisions in my life as it relates to career and lifestyle." Clearing this gate allowed Phoebe to move forward with her exploration of who she wanted to be in light of that decision. "I can make now decisions that I never thought were possible because I have made that one."

Another woman, Sophia, talked about similar gating issues to her own exploration. She was in her mid-fifties, with four sons. "Permission. I finally gave myself permission to pursue *what I wanted*. Permission was about giving myself control to really go figure out what I'd like to do next. You know, when you are putting kids through private college, you don't give yourself permission. You get up, you go to work." Sophia, like many others, had prioritized certain life events, like educating the children, as gates.

The final set of responses regarding the act of decisioning were those in which women experienced events or triggers that provided a laser-like focus, instant clarity. Amy, an early forties account executive, shared a story about when she realized that her terminally ill husband was going to die. She recalled the moment it happened and, while it was tragic, once she acknowledged this reality, it allowed her to make decisions in alignment with this very sad, life-changing truth. While the situation was devastating, she acknowledged that the decision gate allowed her to be different with her husband in the time that remained and begin to reframe her thinking as she looked ahead for herself as a single parent of two young girls.

Each woman processed the decision step differently. Few women focused entirely on this decision. Most considered the decision in parallel with other demanding issues in their lives, like changes in health status or the demands of their jobs or the needs of their children. Sheila, a single woman in her late thirties who had just completed her MBA, said, "I think the harder point is leading up to making the decision to make the transition versus once I have made the decision to leap in it. I beat myself up more leading up to the decision and kind of feel more barriers leading up to making the leap. Leading up, I think, a lot of it is outside expectations of what I should be doing from either parents, society, friends. The real decision requirement for me was being quiet enough to listen to kind of what I actually feel."

Deciding to proceed with transitioning can occur in an instant or over the course of time. Some decisions are event driven, others the product of thinking over the long term. Regardless of the elapsed time, it appeared that women were able to move forward once they made an active informed choice—to initiate an action, the process of transitioning.

Transition's Anatomy

The anatomy of transition is comprised of three segments: a trigger, a decision, and an action. Triggers are multidimensional and nonlinear. Triggers can lead to a decision to transition. The presence of triggers alone does not guarantee such an action. Decisions in support of transitioning are choices. They manifest themselves in many ways, but all require a woman to make an informed choice. The rubric of proceeding through triggers and the decision structures they introduce are highly personal and intertwined with many emotions and thoughts, which is our next topic.

CHAPTER 3

Our Reactions

Our reactions play a significant role in the experience of transition, particularly in and around the triggers that initiate the process. These reactions—made up of emotions, thoughts and feelings—are everywhere. No surprise. What was surprising was women's beliefs about their reactions. Women in my research found it remarkable to learn that other women felt the same way they did. In fact, many women shared that their first response to their transition was, "There must be something wrong with *me*." Solitary. Questioning. Self-limiting?

What are our reactions to transition? Carolyn, a 50-year-old mother of two sons, from San Francisco, described her feelings when she transitioned from full-time work to being full time in the home. "Scared. Absolutely scared. And this feeling of, 'Why did I do this?'" She met me as part of her second transition, prompted by her desire to re-engage in the workforce. "I was mad. I was angry. I was in a strange place for myself—not understanding what was to come."

Is Carolyn's experience representative of other women's? Could our experience of transition be more commonplace than we know? This chapter introduces a common set of reactions identified by women in transition. In fact, I will use the term "emotion" to represent the myriad thoughts, feelings, and emotions that we can ascribe to the three phases of transition: a trigger, a decision, and an action. The chapter also discusses the route or course that these emotions take in one's own experience. The chapter explores as well the risk of misinterpreting emotions and an approach useful in managing them. It concludes with a discussion of risk and its role in transition.

Reactions to Transition

Women experienced a broad range and similar set of emotions in transition. Triggers differed. They ran the gamut: from infertility or job loss or menopause or marriage or restlessness or boredom or much more. Regardless of the triggering event, women seemed to experience the same set of emotions. Even more interesting, emotions seemed to be decoupled from a specific trigger. Anger or empowerment could easily accompany a job loss. So too, a divorce. There was no exclusive pairing between a trigger and its emotions.

The emotions that accompanied transition drew from a broad lot. Anxiety. Fear. Uncertainty. Anger. Embarrassment. Excitement. Inspiration. Freedom. Women shared a rich inventory of positive and negative emotions that accompany transition. Look at the words in Figures 3.1 and 3.2. Women were asked to characterize their transitions. Even though the triggers differed, women cited similar not-so-positive and positive emotions as part of their reaction to transition. While a long list, most women in my research were familiar with nearly all of them.

Women's experience of the emotions in transition tended to move in a cyclical pattern. Sally, a woman whose transition was triggered by her divorce at 41, said, "Scary. Overwhelming. Fragile. And optimistic. I feel lighter now that I have that burden released from me. There are some days when it is overwhelming. Then the next day I'll be energized and hopeful." The path through these emotional states was not linear in any fashion. Just because a woman experienced negative emotions early on did not mean that she was free and clear of negative emotions later as her transition progressed. Negative emotions could be a part of a beginning just as readily as they could be a part of a later stage. If my experience is representative, I observed that the intensity of the negative emotions tended to diminish as more and more positive ones began to be present.

A handful of women with whom I spoke were aware of and shared their thoughts about the cyclical nature of their emotions while in transition. "If I had to do it again, I wouldn't give so much energy to the negative cycles," shared Kerry, a woman who had left a strategic planning role at a well-known consumer packaged goods company. She and her family moved to Chicago following a long stint in Boston. "I am surprised at how personal it was. My experience was long, confusing, and painful."

She described a series of ups and downs, along with a few breakthroughs. "My identity was wound up in working with a prestigious industry-leading organization. Early on I was sad, grieving the loss of that. Then I was up, excited about the new. The ups and downs went back and forth. They felt continuous for a time. It was exhausting. I was reinventing who I wanted to be."

While I was fascinated by the broad range of emotions that accompanied transition, I was more struck by the consistency with which I heard women reference a turning inward during transition. Therese, a dynamic teacher from a private West coast school, said, "I really struggled. I got canned. And it was just—I was so embarrassed. It was really difficult for me to talk about it. And as a matter of fact I lost my job at the end of June. And I didn't tell my mother until Labor Day weekend because I couldn't tell my mother until I could say it without crying." Sandy Anderson, author of *Women in Career & Life Transitions*, observed that women, "swallow up into themselves during challenging times," missing opportunities to leverage friends, family, and networks."[1]

Emotions and Misperception

Emotions play an important role in our transitions. For example, triggers are objective events onto which we import meaning. Emotions therefore help direct our response to events or circumstances and also serve as useful learning tools. By raising our awareness of transition's emotions, we can begin to more actively manage the transition cycle. Yet despite their importance, emotions can be deceiving. I fell victim to misinterpreting emotions early on. It created enough distraction for me that I nearly retreated from my transition.

My biggest fear in transitioning had to do with the isolation that transition might bring. The very thought of it smothered me. I was uncomfortable with the thought of sitting by myself with no where to be in the middle of the workday. My entire working life was characterized by activity and people. Colleagues, peers, customers. My calendar was always full—if not with work commitments, then with quasiwork commitments like participation in professional or community organizations. I had worked six days a week for years—by choice.

Because of this existence, my fear of isolation was palpable, very nearly stopping my decision to proceed with transition. After all, I reasoned, I could easily go get a job. On days when this fear raged unchecked, I reasoned that any job would do as long as it filled my calendar. My list of requirements for my desired job felt extremely pliable on those days. After a few Tuesday mornings home alone, though, I realized that my fear was completely misplaced. I began to see that my career was really an impenetrable barrier that I had erected around myself. Near perfect

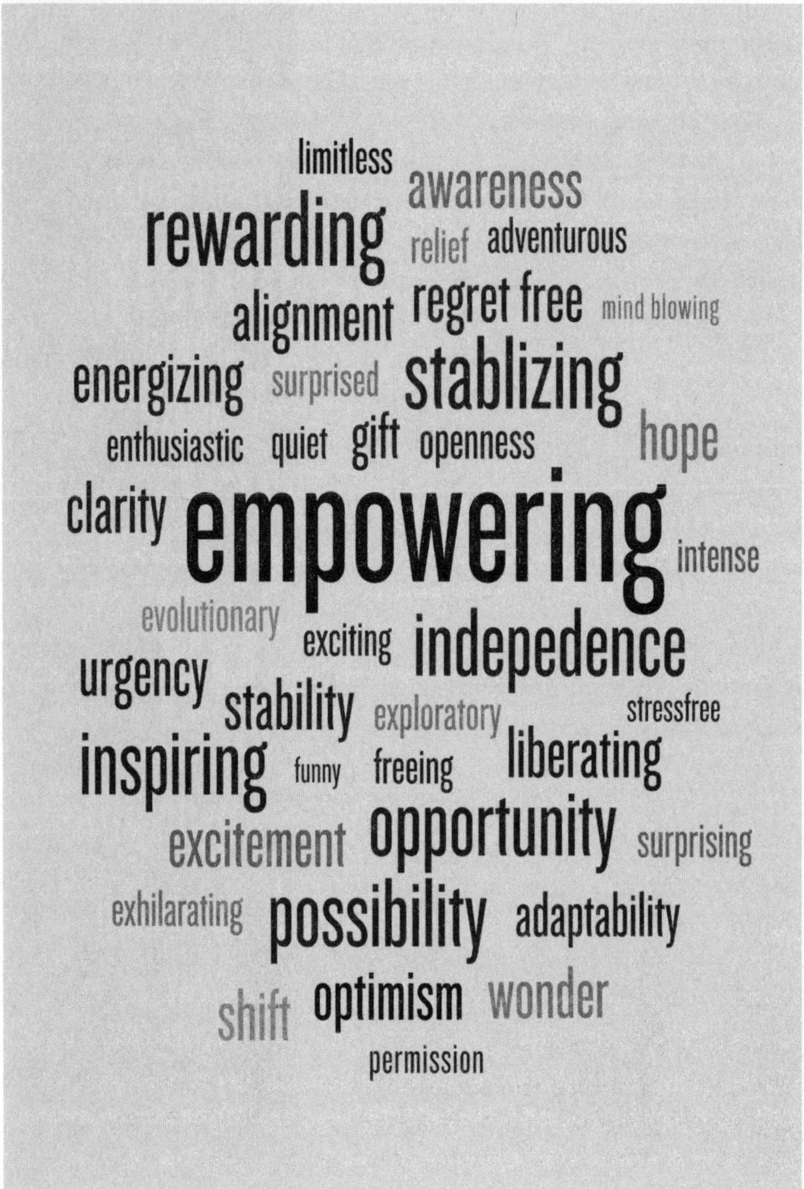

Figure 3.1 Transition's positive reactions.

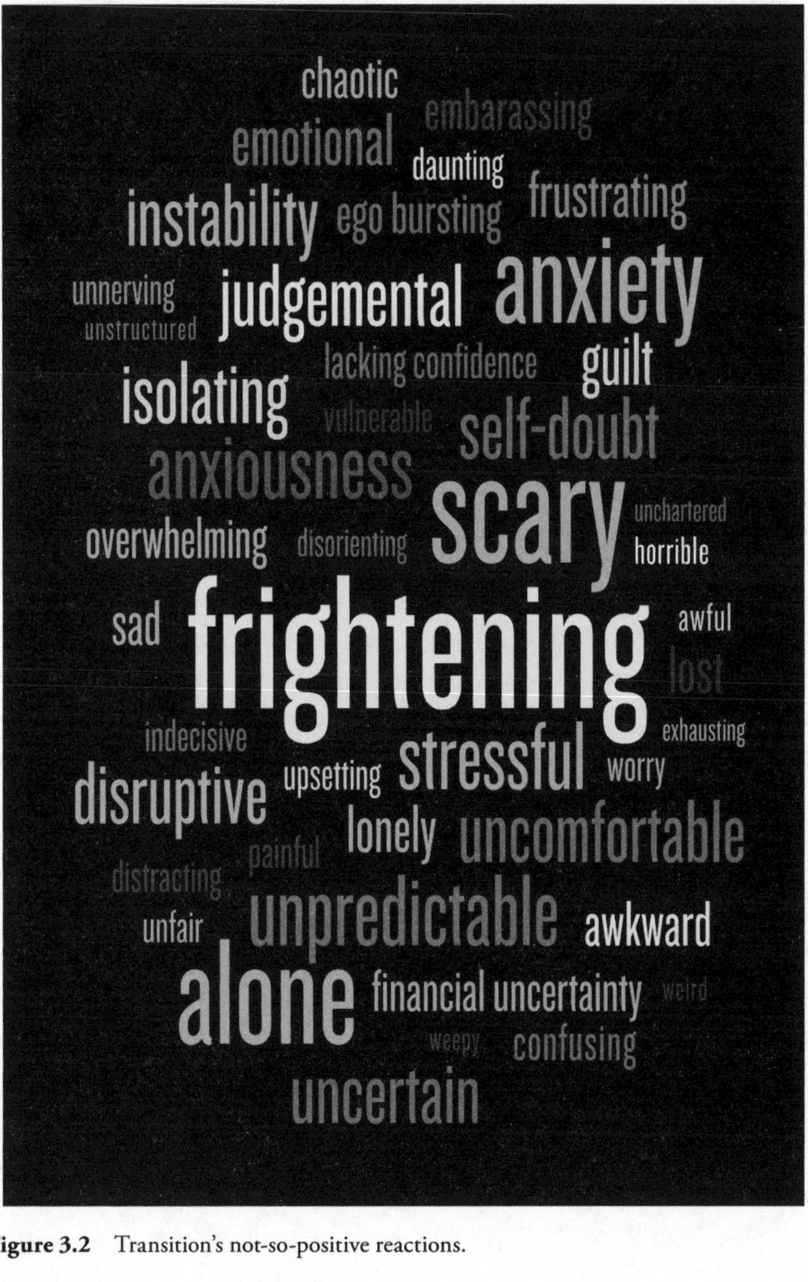

Figure 3.2 Transition's not-so-positive reactions.

isolation. This isolation was fortress-like, constructed with walls of ever-growing 24–7 workplace demands. It blocked me from connecting with almost everyone in my life except my husband and children, whose worlds I parachuted into and out of as regularly as possible. My fear of isolation tricked me. It terrified me as I considered transitioning, and yet I had unknowingly already fallen prey to isolation while working.

My schedule was relentless. I remember one 36-hour cycle. I joined our CEO for a special event on the West Coast one morning. We had been invited to speak at an employee breakfast panel.

After appearing that morning, I would attend a few other meetings on the West Coast with members of my team who were located there and whom I rarely saw in person. Then I would fly to Boston and arrive at 11:30 p.m. Eastern. During the plane ride—a blessed six hours of uninterrupted work time—I would dive into a series of "must-do" tasks that could be queued up for e-mail syncing as soon as the plane landed. Once home, I would log into e-mail to upload some critical communication and then check in on a set of materials queued up by our nanny. The materials were required for the next morning, a morning during which I would take two hours off to join an event at my son's preschool. From there I would head into my office in Boston to connect with members of my team, a team that was spearheading the largest enterprise technology initiative underway in the corporation. After a series of meetings scheduled for the afternoon, I would race back to the suburbs to attend a soccer clinic that both my daughter and son played in on Friday evenings. My life resembled this treadmill every day.

Once in transition I saw that this constant flurry of activity together created nearly complete isolation. I was not aware of how isolated I was in that "very successful" cocoon I had created for myself. It took months of silence on Tuesday mornings for me to realize that the real isolation had occurred for me pretransition. It was absolute. All encompassing. Invisible.

I hope you do not misinterpret my view of the demands of my career and my decision to transition. I observed in speaking with countless women that the commitment level required for jobs like the one I had can only be sustained if the job itself represents something that you *love*. This notion was something that I knew firsthand after running an entrepreneurial start-up, my passion. It was something I wanted to reignite as I looked forward in transition.

Our emotions, including our fears, can play important roles in our transition. If left unexamined, they can cause havoc and lead us to misplaced conclusions about ourselves and our capabilities. But what if we were able to harness the power of them, while reducing the risk of misinterpretation?

Risk and Failure

Another all too frequent theme that emerged from my research was that women often interpreted triggers or the earliest signals of transition as, "I've failed." This response manifested itself in countless ways, like a reaction to an unexpected job loss or a reaction to an unresolved conflict at home or a reaction to a career choice that no longer held one's interest. This failure posture seemed too easily to lead women to false conclusions about their own capabilities. I always struggled when I heard women take this posture. It seemed to drive women to stall, disengage, or retreat from the lives they imagined. My efforts at understanding this dynamic led me to explore failure and risk—two elements at play in transition.

Transitioning requires a person to take on real risk. By choosing transition, we step forward into the unknown. There is enormous uncertainty that surrounds the outcome of this decision. Risk in transition, like elsewhere in life, is present and is not binary. Risk is not simply present or absent. You set the level of risk you are willing to take on in transition. Maybe you are not comfortable re-examining all of the assumptions behind identity, capacity, and values. Perhaps you will start by focusing on one or part of one. Risk can be dialed up or down depending on the decisions you alone make. It is only in the movies that you need to take on reckless levels of risk in order to proceed. You alone are the determinant of the level and type of risk present for you in transition.

I found it incredibly useful to understand the role of risk through its corollary, failure. I turned to a friend for advice just prior to taking on a huge risk. She and I had been at grad school together. She was an industrial engineer and served as a leader in a strategic planning group for an entertainment holding company. I was on the fence about starting a tech company, the one for which I would later raise venture capital and go on to sell to a well-known technology outsourcer. We spoke by phone late one night. She told me a simple story.

Her dad had run for political office in the Washington, DC, area. The punch line is that he did not win the race. Despite this disappointing outcome for her dad, she went on to describe how people treated him differently from that moment onward. It made all the difference in the world…the simple fact that he had put himself out there to try. He acted in a way that was meaningful to him. He was willing to envision a future and articulate that vision to others. Along the way he demonstrated his skills and the things he cared most deeply about. Could he have done more had he been elected? Probably. *Maybe.*

Her message to me that night was that failure was really irrelevant. Her dad's willingness to accept risk made a significant difference for him from that point onward. This story gave me an unexpected gift on the eve of becoming an entrepreneur. I realized that even if I failed, it would likely allow me to continue on a trajectory more important than the one I would be on if I never tried. It neutralized failure for me. Failure was not the failure I had envisioned in my imagination. It was learning that opened me up to possibilities I had not even seen previously. It made me ask, "What is the real risk in transition? Could the real risk be never trying?"

The cycle of risk and failure presents itself to us repeatedly over the course of our lives. Sometimes we do not see it, and other times we see it but choose to ignore it. When we engage, we have the opportunity to grow and learn. By engaging repeatedly we develop a resiliency that I observed countless times in my research. The resiliency in turn allows us to withstand challenges as we make our way through transition. It also builds confidence that we can do it again when faced with new circumstances that may require action. Beneath it all, whether traversing emotions as part of a transition or readying for another transition cycle, resilience emerges from our familiarity with this cycle of risk and failure.

Susan, a woman who had transitioned in the past, offered a story in which her resilience and ability to take risk had come full circle. She had just turned 50. "Regret-free," she said in characterizing her transition. "I knew what I was getting into, and I know that it is totally different from a lot of other people. I made a conscious decision to walk away from a pretty successful career and a lot of money." She was not preachy or boastful. Instead she spoke in a measured fashion, confident and understated. "There was a time when I was getting divorced and I had a serious financial situation. I needed to keep that job. And then I got to the point where I think I've evolved enough as being past the divorce—both financially and emotionally."

Her decision was a clean break. She had no destination in mind. She was able to discuss her objectives, "Getting alignment. I could have definitely stayed on the job and moved up. But it wasn't what I wanted to do."

Her decision was not reckless in any manner. She had been through painful transitions before. She was now choosing to step back into uncertainty. She had a financial cushion that allowed her some freedom. She was making a new commitment.

An Approach

Emotions are simply that, *emotions*. Regardless of the circumstances of one's transition, emotions are not a proxy for our self-worth. If you take nothing else from this book, I hope that you remember that characterization. Emotions can be incredibly powerful and misleading, like my fear of isolation. The reverse is also true—our awareness and understanding of emotions can be energizing and freeing. I have observed too often in speaking with women that, if left unchecked, emotions can fuel feelings of inadequacy and self-doubt. The frequency with which I heard these damaging and false conclusions led me to explore how to manage emotions in such a way as to circumvent this effect.

Maintaining objectivity with respect to emotions seemed to be the key to staying strong despite uncertainty, fear, and many other emotions present for us in transition. Several women whom I met seemed to have the ability to isolate the emotions that accompanied transition. With this skill they were able to minimize the risk of letting those emotions overwhelm them or impede their progress.

How can one maintain objectivity as one is met with all manner of emotions in transition? The uncertainty alone can be crushing. Barbara Kivowitz, psychologist and author of *In Sickness and Health: Helping*

Couples Cope with the Complexities of Illness,[2] shared with me a psychological technique called *externalizing*, which achieves what I describe as objectivity. Externalizing asks users to reposition problems by saying, "The person is not the problem. The problem is the problem." If a woman were angry about her transition, this approach would ask the woman to change adjectives to nouns. So instead of saying, "I am angry," the woman would talk about "how long the anger had been influencing her." According to Kivowitz, psychologists utilize this approach to invite people to objectify the problem as opposed to internalizing it.

Kivowitz also noted that the process of externalizing gives agency or ownership to the person who is experiencing the emotions rather than casting that person as passive or reactive. "It can be powerful in removing negative effects like self-labeling. And it also reduces blame, guilt and shame."[3]

This approach can be useful, because I believe the Holy Grail of emotions in transition lies in a woman's ability to maintain an active versus a passive mental picture. Objectivity helped me interpret emotions like the shame or guilt I felt early on because I was not working 70 hours a week like my "successful" peers. It also helped me parse the real issues behind failure as I started to try new things in the earliest stages of my transitioning process. Emotions are simply that, emotions. How we experience them can determine the energy and belief structure we call upon in transition.

Giving Voice to Emotions in Transition

Some readers will be suspicious about this chapter's opening, in which I cite women and their surprise in finding others who felt the same about emotions and transition. After all, do women not frequently discuss anxiety and shame and empowerment and exhilaration? I believe some of their surprise stemmed from attaching the rubric of transition to their emotions.

We do not as a society have a vocabulary for transition. Ellen Galinsky, president of the Families and Work Institute,[4] was interviewed on this topic when she appeared as a guest on National Public Radio's *The Diane Rehm Show*. Galinsky said, "Everybody thinks of it as a personal problem and that they have to solve that problem (alone)." The lack of vocabulary and a framework leaves many searching to characterize what is going on.

This absence became clearer to me when I caught Carey Goldberg's, former Boston Bureau chief for the *New York Times*, "When You Lose Your Sport, What Happens to Your Self?"[5] It featured a clinical psychologist, Dr. Matthew Krouner, who worked with athletes who transitioned and had to give up their sport(s). Krouner said, "They had to face the monumental challenge of losing an 'all-encompassing identity.'" When was the last time such a description was voiced for a midcareer woman who is forced to step back from her job due to care demands? Maybe she has received news that her elementary school child was diagnosed as having developmental challenges or elder care needs demanded more involvement.

The absence of a vocabulary and a framework for transition seemed to contribute to many women feeling alone in the face of emotions and harboring feelings of inadequacy and self-doubt.

Emotions and Transition

Emotions accompany transition, particularly its triggers. They are common to all transitions. A broad set of emotions are present in transition, although they are not paired specifically with any single triggering event. Emotions move in a cyclical repetitive pattern throughout our transition. Emotions can be instructive. Many women interviewed here voiced misperceptions about emotions and frequently interpreted early signs of transition with a reflexive failure response. Externalizing emotions can be utilized as an approach such that we can learn as much as possible from them. Transition involves risk, but so too breeds a resiliency invaluable to women as they continue on life's course.

As I began to get closer to the emotions present in transition, I could not help but wonder what role knowledge of transition's anatomy might play? Could awareness of transition help us interpret these emotions? Or better yet, redirect our energy toward managing transition's uncertainty? Was this dynamic related to women's transitions or to all transitions? It was time to get closer to understanding the role of gender.

CHAPTER 4

Is Transition Gendered?

A s I met and talked with more and more women, I grew more excited about the definition for transition and the usefulness of its framework. One dimension remained unresolved: *was transition different for women?* I could not pretend as if there was nothing to this question. Women I spoke with constantly added qualifiers to their stories: "part-time," "re-entering," "exiting," or a subtle apology for decisions, like the decision to stay at home full time. Others shared career right turns spawned by unplanned events tied to care roles, like a child's diagnosis with a learning disability or a spouse's illness. The frequency with which I heard comments like these suggested to me that there was something more in transition for women. *But what?*

"I focus on women's development," I offered as about a dozen people went around a long rectangular table introducing themselves. We were kicking off an invitation-only event at an Italian restaurant in the western suburbs of Boston.

Our hosts, attorneys Neil Aronson and Larry Gennari,[1] held these monthly networking dinners as part of their commitment to emerging businesses along the once-storied Route 128 belt.[2] The highway dubbed America's Technology Highway has served as a high-tech emblem in the region for decades, similar to California's Silicon Valley.

"My particular area of focus is women and transition," I quickly added. I wanted to stave off the typical questions I get when I use the term "women's development." Given that I was "in transition," it was not obvious to me why I was on the invitee list. Veteran entrepreneur, perhaps?

"Linda, it's the same for men," Neil chimed in. Everyone chuckled. Next person's turn.

A decade earlier, Neil and I had worked closely together. He had been my lead attorney for the technology start-up that I ran. We secured venture capital together. We executed the sale of the company. He served on my Board of Directors. I trusted his instincts and welcomed the creativity he brought to the table.

Amid the chatter that evening, I could not help but wonder, "The same for men? *Really?*"

At one level I completely understood Neil's perspective. Anyone—female or male—can transition. Despite this truism, I have come to believe that transition is a highly gendered *experience*, but not for the reasons you may think. The obvious reasons lie with a woman's reproductive capacity. Let us face it. Our physiology itself can generate events that could trigger a transition. Childbirth. Menopause. Infertility. Miscarriage. While each of these can be a valid transition trigger, none satisfied my curiosity.

My hypothesis was that transition is gendered because of women's response to it, a response that is guided by how women are socialized. Our socialization impacts who we are. By definition, socialization is "the lifelong process of inheriting and disseminating the norms, customs, and ideologies that provide an individual with the skills and habits necessary for participating within her society."[3] Women's socialization contributes three important factors that have an influence on transition. These are the presence and authenticity of our voices; our access to reliable sources of recognition; and our belief structure about what we could or should do and how we define success. This chapter explores each of the three and concludes with a discussion of why this matters to transition.

Discomfort with Gender

I feel as if I have spent my entire life proving that gender differences do not exist—from the workplace, to my home, to the myriad community groups in which I participate. I believe through to my core that gender differences are irrelevant in thinking about one's capacity or one's ability to contribute. In my mind, anyone can do anything they put their mind and heart to. I demonstrate this belief in everything I do, particularly in how I parent my daughter and my son. I hope you can imagine, therefore, just how difficult it is for me to take the position that the experience of transition—a woman's response to it—is highly gendered because of women's socialization.

In researching this book, I encountered a broad and evolving school of thought about gender. The most forward thinkers in this arena consider gender to be a collection of masculine and feminine traits independent of one's anatomy or physiology. I cannot do justice here to this complex and far-ranging school of thought. For the purposes of this discussion, I rely on more traditional constructs of gender, acknowledging that it has limitations.

In fact, thanks to my personal compass, I was not sold on the notion of transition being a gendered experience at the outset of my journey. I am thankful for my disbelief, however, because it made me more careful in my exploration and ultimately more confident in my conclusion: "*Yes, Neil, gender plays a significant role in transition.*" Here is why.

Women's Socialization and Voice

Has a female friend or family member ever said to you, "I don't know what I want to do next?" As I started talking with women, I heard this statement or something like it countless times. A common derivative was, "I finally have the time, but I don't know what I want to do." It was present at retirement as frequently as it was at a transition triggered by the birth of a child. It was present after personal tragedies like the death of a loved one as well as for women who proactively sought midcareer moves. It was present for me when I finally paused for a moment after decades of 24–7 dedication to the business world. Why was it that so many women, including myself at times, struggled in conjuring their own voice?

What is voice? Voice is the oral representation of that which is meaningful to you. It is fundamental in transition. It serves as an asset. An enabler. Voice directs our response to the re-examination of assumptions that lie at the heart of transition. It serves as a vehicle through which we articulate what we want or hope to achieve.

Research into this area has linked women's socialization with voice. In *Meeting at the Crossroads: Women's Psychology and Girls' Development*, authors Lyn Mikel Brown and Carol Gilligan conducted longitudinal research and found that our socialization impacts women's and girls' voices in meaningful ways.[4] They noted that connections with others, or relationships, are a "central organizing feature in women's development."[5] Their research was inspired by a deep-seated conflict they heard in speaking with both women and men. Women spoke of their connection to relationships, but at the very same time they described a "giving up of voice"[6] in order to maintain those relationships. They observed, as girls became women they were more willing to "silence themselves in relationships,"[7] rather than risk loss of such a relationship. What exactly did it mean, "to silence themselves"? Silencing one's voice was akin to hitting a mute button. It was a learned behavior meant to achieve a relationship objective.

As girls become young women, the researchers also observed that they "dismiss their experience and modulate their voices,"[8] in favor of what they believe to be expected or acceptable to the relational environment within which they find themselves. In studying second- through eleventh-grade girls, Mikel Brown and Gilligan observed a tendency on the part of the girls to voice over their true feelings. The older girls did not base decisions necessarily on what they themselves wanted. Instead they had learned how to filter or ignore their own wants and needs. Older girls based their decisions on "what other people wanted" or "what other people felt."[9] Mikel Brown and Gilligan concluded that the socialization that affects voice eventually can create a dynamic in which girls and women do not know their "own thoughts and feelings."[10]

Even though I found Mikel Brown and Gilligan's research captivating, I wanted to believe that it was dated and no longer valid. Sadly, what I heard from women in my research reinforced these 20-year-old findings. From the women I interviewed, I too often heard statements like, "I'm finally valuing what I want, instead of what someone else wants for me."

How could this be? In the 20 years since *Meeting at the Crossroads* was published, we have invested in confidence and self-esteem in women and girls. Everything from field hockey teams to the Girl Scouts speaks of empowering young women. Women have even surpassed men in the attainment of baccalaureate degrees—with women receiving 56.7 percent of all bachelor's degrees in 2013.[11] And yet as I write this, the *New York Times'* "Corner Office" column interviewed four very accomplished female leaders. The topic? "Finding and Owning Their Voice."[12]

When my transition began, I realized that I was not immune to this loss of voice. Do not get me wrong. I am not a shy and retiring type. I always speak up, but what I share has always gone through a rigid filter. I remember sitting one afternoon in the office of a colleague and mentor. He asked energetically, "So, what do you want to do?" I responded with, "I don't know." It was as if the air escaped from his balloon. His mood changed. He replied, "Are you going away from something or toward something?" Tears instantly welled up in my eyes. I was not sure how to answer him nor was I sure why it made me cry. Could it be for the first time I realized I really did not know?

At the time, I had been listening to a series of TED Radio Hour interviews on NPR.[13] One caught my attention because it spoke to the potential, extreme long-term effects of diminished voice. A not-for-profit leader, Jacqueline Novogratz, observed that those who diminish or extinguish their voice for a period of time may have trouble reconjuring it. Why? She said that after a while "it's really hard to say what you mean mostly because people never really ask you and when they do, you don't think they really want to know the truth."[14]

Could women's socialization influence not only our ability to access voice but also the authenticity of our voice? Through socialization, women are too often schooled via implicit social cues to diminish, distrust, or overwrite their own voice, a practice that we will later see can make the initial stages of transitioning difficult.

Women's Socialization and Recognition

This next area is a tricky one for me. *Recognition.* Would it surprise you that there are dimensions to recognition that evolve from how women are socialized? Like many of us, I struggle with being singled out for what I contribute. It takes a village after all. Let us just say that I would grade myself poorly on what authors Deborah Kolb, Judith Williams, and Carol Frohlinger, authors of *Her Place at the Table*, state is a nonnegotiable for women: "make value visible."[15] With value come recognition and other social and psychological rewards.

Researchers have found that being recognized for something plays a role in our ability to envision a future for ourselves. Our bodies respond to recognition is basic ways. Anna Fels, psychiatrist, researcher, and author of the 2004 *Necessary Dreams: Ambition in Women's Changing Lives*, said, "Recognition is formative and enlivening. It is the motivational engine that allows one to develop what is required to pursue ambition. From a biological perspective, recognition increases the production of energizing confidence enhancing neurotransmitters."[16] In other words, our bodies respond at a fundamental level to recognition.

The frequency with which women receive recognition is influenced by our socialization. Fels concluded that "a deep and pervasive cultural prejudice leads to the reflex of bestowing recognition on males and largely unconscious withholding of recognition from females in all but the sexual sphere."[17] She went on to say that this is "a form of discrimination while not as obvious as being denied the right to vote or receiving less pay for equal work,"[18] but one that has profound implications on women's advancement. Fels said that "women who do not formulate life plans that are supported by appreciative communities pay a steep price. They often fail to understand why, in the absence of such affirmation, they feel unmotivated and demoralized. They blame it on their lack of discipline or character or talent. But if sources of recognition are unavailable or inadequate or outside a woman's control, the chances are dim that she will thrive in her chosen enterprise."[19]

The lens of recognition offered me a new look at a series of decisions I had made leading up to my transition. About two years into my C-suite role, the demands of my role were getting more and more intense. My youngest was almost three at the time. I resigned from a not-for-profit board on which I chaired the Finance and Strategic Planning Committees. I withdrew from professional and social commitments. I gave up the occasional dinner or coffee with a friend. Why? I reasoned—incorrectly—that I could not spare another night away from my family. Already I was spending inordinate amounts of time away from my very young children. How could I sacrifice another night out to attend a meeting or event?

What I did not know at the time was that these commitments were important sources of recognition for me. The other thing that I missed was that at work and at home I was the supporter, the ubersupporter of everyone else. In light of this, my decision to withdraw from many commitments was costly. I had few intact spheres of support or recognition. It was no wonder that I was running on empty. My decision to withdraw from commitments, while intended to keep my head above water, only served to do the reverse.

Women's Socialization, Male Norms, and Care Roles

It may not surprise you that there are many environmental factors at play as we re-examine our assumptions in transition. Our socioeconomic, educational, racial, ethnic, and cultural backgrounds are all present. What might not be so obvious, but is nonetheless a significant factor, is the influence of our male-normed environment. I have learned that this factor plays a role in how we view "what we could do," or "what we should do," and—perhaps most importantly—how we define "success."

Prior to starting this project, I was unaware of the term "male normed." I have worked in and contributed to many large organizations that were predominantly male. Even so, I would never have used the term male normed.

My research taught me to look at this subject more carefully. Joan C. Williams, in her book *Reshaping the Work-Family Debate: Why Men and Class Matter*[20] observed that it is masculinity and masculine norms in the workplace that shape opportunities for everyone there and throughout society. Her research revealed these norms have been established over decades by assumptions about what it means to be masculine and the attractiveness of the traits—like "independence, ambition, and competitiveness,"[21]—associated with it. Williams, an attorney and expert on families, gender, and the law, argued that the high value placed on men and masculine traits leads to expectations of what it means to be successful in both work and social settings.

Sandra Lipsitz Bem, author of the 1993 *The Lenses of Gender: Transforming the Debate on Sexual Inequality,*[22] took it further than Williams. She said that the real issues with male norms lie with their influence on what we view as *standard* in our society. Standard in her work was linked to, "Hidden assumptions about gender embedded in cultural discourses, social institutions, and individual psyches that invisibly and systematically,"[23] bestow privilege to males and male experience. Bem offered numerous examples of these unquestionable standards, like the mismatch between the workday and the school day, or the virtual lack of availability of part-time work.

I found a lighthearted yet insightful example of the invisibility and power of male norms in our workplaces in Williams's *Why Men Work So Many Hours.*[24] She said, "Way back when I was a visiting professor at Harvard Law School, I used to call it the cult of busy smartness. How do the elite signal to each other how important they are? '*I am slammed*' is a socially acceptable way of saying, '*I am important.*'"[25] Williams believes that the message conveyed by this phrase was less about schedule and more about workplace norms. We elevate those who work such hours. Williams argues that it is our modern day expression of virility. Workplaces hold these behaviors in high regard, which in turn solidifies their influence throughout organizations. "Workplace norms cement felt truths that link long hours with manliness, moral stature and elite status."[26] Dislodging these truths is extraordinarily difficult and far exceeds our efforts to date in addressing the gender issue with programmatic solutions like flexible work hours or parental leave. Williams's concludes, "It's not productivity,"[27] but rather a cultural issue that affects all employees in the economy.

I remember one Friday afternoon when I confronted these male norms head-on. My kids visited me in my office. They were probably three and five at the time. One of my C-suite colleagues happened to be walking by my office shortly after they arrived. On seeing my children, he stepped in to say hello. My daughter, who was older and quite a bit taller than my son at the time, was closest to the door. My son was several steps away.

I will never forget what happened next. My colleague reached around my daughter to shake my son's hand first. Only after that was complete did he step back to shake my daughter's hand. I stood there in disbelief. What did his behavior say about felt truths in that environment or in society at large? Could this event have been another —even earlier—trigger for my transition?

If we focus on the intersection of male norms and care roles, which are largely populated by women and a growing but small number of men, we encounter significant unresolved conflicts. What role does this lack of resolution play in our beliefs about what we should or could do, or how we define success? I am not sure how to answer that question, but I can say that the number of people influenced by this issue is large. A November 2014 poll of nonworking adults aged 25–54 in the United States, sponsored by the *New York Times*/CBS News/Kaiser Family Foundation, found that the majority of female respondents, or 61 percent, said family responsibilities were a reason they were not working.[28] In another sample, the Census Bureau reported that over the last decade, the participation rate of women in the US workforce has declined for the first time in six decades, a decline of 5 percent at a cost of close of ten million jobs.[29] While staggering, these statistics do not account for the widespread underemployment of women that is caused by their need to reconcile their care roles and their workplace roles. Often this latter group trades quality jobs for flexibility—as flexibility takes precedence over many other factors when care roles are at play.

Regina, a Southern California native in her early forties, shared her perspective. She had graduated from a well-regarded college and worked as a product marketing manager for several years. We met for coffee at an artsy shop in downtown Pasadena. She told me of the unexpected transition she had gone through about a decade earlier.

When she was expecting her first baby, she said, "there was a lot of pressure on me to buy into the concept of being a full-time mother." Her husband, her in-laws, and her own parents voiced strong opposition to her continuing to work full time after the baby was born. Yet she never considered not working prior to having children, even though she and her husband really wanted a family. It was one of the reasons she loved him— his desire to build a family together.

Regina and her husband believed that financially they would be ok on one salary. That decision neutralized any financial motivators in favor of her continuing to work.

Regina's options as she considered transition were highly influenced by the unresolved nature of the conflict between our care roles and our male-normed society. "I was the guilty party for wanting to pursue my work. It was a particularly difficult time."

She ultimately decided to exit the workforce. Her decision was one that she described as "scary." At the time, she did not believe there was a good option for her. The input of those around her left her feeling as if she did not really have an option.

Does Our Socialization Matter to Transition?

As I tried to understand the gendered nature of transition, my research led me to consider how our socialization might influence our response to transition. It influences the presence and authenticity of our voices; our access to reliable sources of recognition; and our belief structure about what we could or should do, or how we think about success.

The influence of these factors is important because in transition we will be asked to *respond* to a number of things. At every point in transition's anatomy—the triggers, decisions, or actions—we respond. At the moment we encounter a job loss or an empty nest, this socialization helps frame what we believe to be possible. This influence can shape how we view our options at the moment we begin transitioning or even well before that as we try to interpret a trigger or decide how to proceed.

Is Transition Gendered?

Transition itself is not gendered. Our response to it is, though, thanks, in large part to how we are socialized.

My hope is that by raising your awareness of these influences, you become better able to recognize them and any potential bias that they could introduce for you. This awareness will not fix the structural issues facing women every day nor the cultural inertia that seems to enable so much of it. However, awareness can help us reframe our thinking. It can empower us to reach forward with renewed energy—focused on the unique possibility that resides within each of us.

For my part, I used this awareness in designing the action steps we need to take in transitioning. The process that is introduced in the next section integrates several countermeasures—like a strong focus on voice —targeted at the very issues that may be present for women due to our socialization.

SECTION 2

The Mechanics of Transitioning

CHAPTER 5

A Process Overview

I emerged from my work on understanding transition with a tremendous data set and a newfound belief about the importance of transition. The possibility for transition was everywhere. Emotions surrounded it. Few discussed it. I was certain, thanks to my discovery work, that transition represented an enormous opportunity for women. It was immediately apparent that transition inspired women. It left them energized and exhilarated. I rarely heard of women for whom it did not offer something meaningful—like courage or confidence or peace. I felt enormous gratitude in my own life for what this understanding had introduced to me. Without searching for it—in fact nearly missing it—transition had given me a gift. With this gift and an unshakable belief in transition's value for women, I knew immediately how I could best share my learnings with other women.

I would create a toolkit for women transitioning so that more women could realize transition's value. The usefulness of this toolkit approach became even clearer to me one afternoon after a one-on-one interview I conducted with Michele, a highly successful entrepreneur in her late fifties who lived in upstate New York. We met in an old, slightly tattered diner. She was sharp and well put together. I loved her energy. Michele had transitioned twice over more than two decades. "I did not set out to search for my authentic self," said Michele. "I set out for what gets me out of bed in the morning," she continued. Michele was referring to her first transition, which involved an intentional decision to leave the full-time workforce. She had three school-aged sons at the time. One son was struggling in school. He had just gotten a diagnosis of a learning disability. She and her husband agreed that Michele would quit her job to allow her to spend more time involved in their son's education. "I was afraid of being a full-time mom. I didn't know my identity outside the cloak of title, paycheck, and client. The hardest part was being 37 and not making my own salary."

Michele re-engaged in the workforce after all of her sons had gone to college. She emphasized that every one of them had done so, even and most especially the son whose needs triggered her first transition. Her second transition involved her starting a commercial baking company. While different in some respects from her first, she described her second transition as just as hard. It was uncertain. Frightening. "Maybe not as lonely," she added. "It was important for my sons to watch me not give up."

When I asked her to talk about transition's gifts, she said, "I was surprised. I did not expect to change as much as I did. I realize now that I was offered a chance to find out who I really was. The transition process has given me a generosity of spirit I would never have found." Michele is a big believer in transition. "Fear held me back from both transitions. I am a completely different person. I found love."

Michele's story deepened my belief in transition's value and the usefulness of educating women about it. I wanted to create a process, a transitioning process, through which women could envision and realize a future of their own design. It would need to demystify transition and make it broadly accessible. It would need to be practical and flexible enough to withstand the pressures of women's modern-day existence. It would have to incorporate the highly personal assumptions that underlie transition, while offering sure-footed techniques to help women move forward.

This chapter introduces this Transitioning Process. I highlight four issues that greatly influenced the design of the process. I also talk about two choices women need to make in initiating the process: scope and timing. The chapter concludes with an important transition exercise, a readiness assessment.

The Transitioning Process: An Introduction

Michele's transition's value statement, summarized by, "I found out who I really am," motivated me. In response I created The Transitioning Process, a structured approach designed to assist women in articulating and in realizing their dreams. It has two objectives: to help women imagine the biggest idea possible that will engage their hearts and minds, and to support them as they proceed through cycles of testing and learning to realize these ideas.

The Transitioning Process helps women develop a hypothesis about themselves and their future. Hypothesis is a funny word. Many of us have not used it since fourth-grade science class. It means "an idea or theory that is not proven but that leads to further study or discussion."[1] For our purposes, hypothesis is an idea, a dream, or a wish. Some women with whom I have worked like to think of it as a personal strategy for their future. Others were more comfortable thinking about it using terms like, a future goal. Others liked passion. Regardless of the vocabulary, the process challenges women to explore and question assumptions. Some assumptions, in fact, may be fundamental to how we have defined meaning in our lives up until this exploration.

The entire process is designed to help women define their future selves on their own terms. There is no judgment on my part regarding the appropriateness of your "terms." Some women I met desperately wanted to be a CEO. Others wanted to re-establish alignment between who they were and the many demands placed on their time by work, family, and so much else. Others wanted to re-examine their priorities after a devastating personal event. Still others were struggling to recalibrate their assumptions after a prolonged absence from the workforce. Others were readying for a full-time commitment to parenting. The process works regardless of the terms you define as long as it is based on terms that are entirely *your own*.

What will a woman get at the end of the process? Ideally she will get exactly what Michele got—an introduction to who she really is. This can express itself in intangibles like Michele's love or generosity of spirit. It can also express itself in more tangible ways like a new job or a new spouse. Regardless of your target outcome, my process differs from Michele's in a few important ways. Whereas Michele's process was evolutionary in nature, the Transitioning Process allows women to achieve the very same outcome through a guided, informed cycle. Women who engage in my process also define their own pace and the scope of their transition. Perhaps the most meaningful departure of the process from Michele's evolutionary work is that it addresses some of the most daunting tasks— like envisioning our future selves—by relying on a highly structured set of activities. This approach was designed to facilitate a more thorough

Figure 5.1 The transitioning process.

exploration and mitigate some of the difficulty inherent in trying to think about our own futures.

The Transitioning Process has two phases: Envision and Validate. Underlying these is a refinement loop that serves as a supporting infrastructure for the two phases (see Figure 5.1).

The Envision Phase is all about the internal exploration that accompanies transition: the dreams or assumptions or values that serve as the cornerstone to who we are. The objective of the Envision Phase is to help a woman create a hypothesis about her fullest self anchored by what holds meaning to her alone. I observed that many women shortchange this step, perhaps because of its difficulty. I remember reading about the hypothesis that stood behind the founders of Google in Steven Levy's *In the Plex: How Google Thinks, Works, and Shapes Our Lives.*[2] The founders's dream was to index all of the Internet's pages. It was not to create a search engine. The founders anchored on their dream, and they kept reimagining how to do it. Again and again and again. Along the way they brought on more and more curious people who helped them figure it out. And, voila! They created something enormous and broader than they had actually envisioned at the start. The work of Envision is largely the same. Envision helps women create an individually meaningful and empowering hypothesis like "indexing all of the Internet's pages," by breaking it down into four simple steps.

The Validate Phase helps women test their hypothesis in an informed, data-driven manner. It is made up of four individual tools. A woman works with the tools to test and reconsider her hypothesis. Validate's objective is to assist a woman in refining her vision of herself into a practical, realizable reality.

The refinement loop serves as a check step in the process. It reminds women to listen carefully to themselves and to the input of others as they proceed through transitioning. Refinement cycles help us re-examine our initial hypotheses and improve upon them. Through refinement, women may alter their initial thinking and re-engage in validation or envisioning activities. Women may go through the refinement loop again and again until their outcome is both comfortable and aligned with who they are or wish to become.

The Transitioning Process can be used in different ways. Some will use the process as a map and follow its step-by-step directions. Others will utilize the process to understand more about what transitioning entails. For them the Transitioning Process will serve as an awareness engine deepening their understanding of transition. In whatever way you use the tool, keep in mind that it was created based upon my experience and the experience of women and experts who agreed to assist me with it. The process does not preclude women from working with other contributors, like analysts or career or life coaches. It does however ensure that those without access to such resources can be successful.

Four Stories

The design of the process emerged from my own transition work and from the input of many women and experts who were willing to road-test its components. Four stories serve as illustrations of its key design considerations. The stories highlight specific women's needs during transition. During transition women need to be: future focused versus past focused; anchored by a comprehensive view of identity; mindful of a women's reluctance to reach beyond our comforts and respectful of the very real constraints that characterize most women's daily lives. These four helped me create a process that could be useful and stand up to the real-world issues women face every day.

The process's first design consideration was the need to be future focused versus past focused, a dynamic I refer to as forward looking. Sounds simple, *forward looking*. This was important to me for two reasons. I nearly missed the opportunity to transition in any substantive way.

And I met many women for whom this topic, the future, served as a gate. I wondered why. Too difficult? Too amorphous? Too self-centered? Or perceived as too much of a luxury given all of life's other demands?

I can't count how many times people asked me, "What will you do?" at my transition's beginning. Often our first reaction to questions like this one is to look at what has been successful in the past. That was the first place I looked. I remember sitting in my boss's office just before starting my transition. We were spit balling—his term—ideas about what I might do next. This exercise was a no-risk brainstorming approach that he loved. "You should start a company," he half-chirped, "to establish SEC-compliant processes for pre-IPO companies." In filing to go public, companies are required to file disclosure statements with the Securities and Exchange Commission (SEC). In these statements, companies detail many internal processes, including the granddaddy of them all, the processes that govern the granting of incentive stock options to employees. In the time I had worked for the company, my team had rearchitected many of these processes, including those that govern the granting of employee stock options.

"You really should do that," he said as he was getting more and more animated. "It would be enormously valuable to the companies, and it would likely be very lucrative." Like me, he had also been an entrepreneur prior to his large corporate stint. He loved that arena, and in the years since we worked together he has returned to that environment as the CEO of a pre-IPO (initial public offering) company. In helping me spit ball ideas, my colleague looked at my immediate past for an answer to the question "what next?"

Why dwell on that exchange with my former boss? In the quiet moments after leaving my job, I considered starting that exact business. I reasoned that I could easily do it. His assumptions about it being financially rewarding were likely true. I could also be very good at it because I had had previous start-up experience. There was a valid market for the service even though the IPO market was cyclical in nature. At the time, I could go all through the rationales that would lead to a "yes" decision to start that business.

Wind the clock forward 24 months, and I would not give that idea the time of day. Now I choose to combine my business experience with issues that are more connected to who I am. Thankfully, I altered my direction. I was on the precipice, however, of proceeding in a direction that was decoupled from something very important to me, like women's development. Yes, it aligned with very real skills that I could easily demonstrate. But did it have anything to do with who I was or what I wanted? Was it another expression of someone else's belief of what I could or should do?

This experience underscored the importance of valuing the past but not being limited by it. The process would need to value our past experiences—those that make us unique contributors—and yet provide a framework that allowed women to look forward.

The second design consideration was informed by my growing appreciation of identity and the influence it had on women in the early part of transition. Prior to my own experience with transition, I had not included identity as I thought about the need to make changes in my life. I viewed identity as fixed. I was not aware of the societal expectations all around me that shaped my understanding of what I could or should do.

Identity's role stayed silent for me until a friend called it out. One Monday morning about a year into my transition, I spoke with a friend, Marni. She and I often touched base by phone early in the week because we were both working nontraditional jobs. She was an engineer who chose to leave her full-time position and work part time as a contractor after her kids were born. She had two high school-aged children. Her initial switch away from full-time work happened not because of the children but because of some demanding care issues in her extended family. Even though her initial reason to leave full-time work was resolved, she never returned to it.

"You are really struggling with the identity thing," she said after listening patiently to me tell her about an incident that had occurred the prior weekend. I was a bit embarrassed by her remark. I wanted to say, "What identity thing?" Up until that moment I had not really thought about identity explicitly or its role in my transition.

The prior weekend my husband and I had participated in a community service day that was held in the basement of a church in our town. At the day's outset, all attendees did an ice-breaking exercise. Teams of two had to introduce one another to the other attendees. My husband and I went first. He started with, "This is my wife, Linda. She's a great mom."

I was furious at this. Truth be told, I was insulted by his introduction. Please do not get me wrong. I am a great mom to my two children. They mean the world to me. I give a lot of myself to motherhood and derive a HUGE amount of pleasure from it. But it is not the sole source of my identity. I realize that I may not be representative of every woman. I also make no judgment about those women for whom parenting is their heart's greatest expression. I applaud them for making that choice—hoping always that it is *their* choice.

Let us face it. My husband could have started off with something else. How about C-suite refugee or start-up junkie? Or my current pursuits, like "a contract consultant" or even "a blogger"? He could have tried humor. A joke about my being another underemployed MBA? No. "She is a great mom." I do not recall whether he said much more. I could not hear anything else even though I was only three feet away from him.

My anger that day—although directed at my husband—was more likely a reflection of just how unglued I was about losing my identity. Just who was I?

Telling people that I was in transition did not hold any meaning. If I had introduced myself that morning, I would probably have stumbled through an introduction laced with my past selves. Marni was my ballast that day. Blessedly. I was not sure whether I heard experience or resignation in her voice. I did not really matter. She hit it. Identity. *That identity thing.* Up until that point I had not been aware of the powerful impact identity had on my experience of transition and on how I viewed my choices.

The third issue that I prioritized in the process's design was capacity and its intersection with women's reluctance to reach beyond their comfort zone. A conversation at a Focus Group one evening cemented for me the importance of this topic. That evening, nine women gathered in a conference room at a suburban law firm. We talked while everyone ate salads and deli sandwiches. The conversation was pretty typical except for one comment. An attendee, Grace, a divorced woman in her late forties, had lost her job due to downsizing after a 17-year run as a marketing professional. Over the years she had given enormous amounts of herself to the job, frequently stepping in to respond to emergency requests. She was angry and sad about being laid off. She characterized her transition as "frightening."

As the evening went on, Grace told us about an entrepreneurial project she was developing. Her face lit up as she described it. It captivated her. Then she lobbed in the heartbreaker. "I couldn't think of an adjective, but it feels like it's grandioser than what I'm meant to or allowed to do."

Everyone was silent. Her comment hung in the air. We heard it and its implied limitation. Grace was not alone in this thinking. I was struck by how often I heard stories of women who voiced something similar—a gate standing in the way of a reach, or a limited belief in what might be possible for themselves. Truth be told, I was always uncomfortable while listening to these stories. From my seat, women's reluctance to reach was a tragedy, an avoidable one.

The final issue that influenced the design of the process was my desire to have the process respect the long list of constraints I heard voiced by women. A constraint, if defined as a limitation or restriction, can be anything. Women identified financial or economic constraints, time constraints, physical limitations or health-related constraints, family obligations, the absence of support and even, or especially, themselves. By any measure the list of constraints was lengthy, and sometimes it felt like we were not willing to voice them honestly. Janelle, an exuberant single woman from Detroit, said, "One thing I would say is I think financial barriers are something that a lot of people *say* it's not a barrier (to transition) but it really is. I would live my life a lot more differently if I had no financial barriers. I mean it would be a totally different life. I would go to India and study yoga for, you know, probably for a good year and a half. I don't know, I would just make different choices. So, I think that's real for me. I also feel like, being 40 years old, I feel enormous pressure to have kids now."

Constraints represented an interesting challenge as I thought about transitioning. Did they represent a gating issue, one that held women back from transitioning? Was transition for the lucky few? My data said otherwise. I concluded that it would be foolish to try to create a process that would ignore the constraints. I also believed that it would be almost as foolish to create one that attempted to fix them. Instead, the process would need to work in the presence of constraints, real-life issues that face all of us.

Design Inspiration: Agile Methodology

Admittedly a quirky idea, I used a business model as an inspiration piece for the Transitioning Process. Similar to House & Garden television's *Renovation Raiders*,[3] in which people choose unexpected objects like vases to guide the redesign of entire rooms, I utilized the Agile Software Development Methodology[4] as an inspiration for the Transitioning Process. For those unfamiliar with Agile, it is a philosophy that got its start in 2001 with a group of forward-thinking technologists who were frustrated with the then-prevailing project management approach to software development known as waterfall. Using waterfall, a project would move sequentially through steps—step 1 to step 2 to step 3. Teams typically differed between steps. Valuable learning from any one step would often be lost in the handoff to the next step's team. This approach led to costly redos, delays, and frustration.

Agile is a complete reversal from waterfall. Agile breaks down a large project into smaller mini-projects that are worked on in continuous short-term cycles. It keeps the energy and focus on near-term instead of on long-term deliverables. Agile also embraces iteration or or adaptive learning cycles, a process by which teams stop during and after each mini-project to assess how to do things better or differently the next time around. Agile relies as well upon stories as a means of conveying information among teams and their participants.

Agile was particularly interesting to me as a model for transition because of its continuous adaptive structure. This structure paved the way as to how one could incorporate continuous minor adjustments and failure while still moving forward. By incorporating this model into transitioning, I found a way to introduce real-life experiences—like failure—into the overall process.

I realize that many people bristle at the sound of even minor failure. Failure even in small increments is an uncomfortable subject. I found another business construct helpful in thinking through failure. Harvard Business School professor and author of *The Innovator's Dilemma*,[5] Clay Christensen, said, "93% of original strategies fail."[6] He went on to add that "companies who win do so not because they had a brilliant initial strategy but because they can iterate quickly."[7] Successful companies are not stopped by failure. Instead they regroup and reflect on what they have learned and then immediately try again. Christensen argued that "strategy is not a discrete analytical event but rather a continuous, diverse, and unruly process."[8] So too transition?

A Word about Timing and Scope

I often get questions about how long it takes to transition. The honest answer is, *it depends*. Once a woman decides to proceed with transition, she needs to decide how much of herself to evaluate, the scope, and how quickly she would like to move through the steps, the pace.

Scope relates to the breadth of issues a woman decides to address in transition. A woman can explore her assumptions about identity, capacity, and values—or any subset of these. In fact, many women in my research were able to identify some assumptions that were outdated and others that were fully aligned with where they were. In Envision, the process requires you to look at all three even though your interest may be only in one or in portions of one or more. Once you complete Envision, you can decide how broadly to engage with Validation based upon what you uncover about yourself.

The second decision a woman needs to make once she initiates transition is the pace at which she will step through the process. The Process is designed to be flexible such that a woman can set her own speed. Once the decision is made to proceed, the pace can be variable.

The process is modular by design. I wanted to remove any process-related barriers that could stand in the way of a woman *beginning*. I was particularly attuned to those women who were so time starved that they could only work on this weekly for one hour at 11 p.m. on a Tuesday evening.

In addition to being modular, the two phases differ in their time commitment. Envision tends to encompass work that can be done alone. Validate relies more on outreach and connection to others. That said, many of these activities can be done via technology. Users can easily swap a Skype call for an in-person breakfast meeting in the Validate Phase. Women will need to define their own pace, given the very real responsibilities we each have in our lives like children or mortgages or health issues. Each of these and many more can impact pace. What is the one nonnegotiable? That we begin.

I cannot emphasize enough the importance of beginning. Stopping or deferring the process altogether introduces real risks to women. I deferred unknowingly for many years. The suspension occurred after I sold the tech start-up company that I had been involved with. After that transaction I buried myself in events or distractions for close to a decade. Some events were incredibly meaningful, like the birth of my two children. Others, not so much. My suspicion is that it took me longer to execute the earlier steps of transitioning than it should have because I had suspended this type of work for so long. Had I kept some level of inquiry going, I would have had an easier time beginning. Instead I was mired in distractions. Eleanor Roosevelt in her 1933 gem, *It's Up to the Women,* said, "We (women) should be able to realize that making up our minds as to what gives us the greatest amount of pleasure and then working for it, is one of the (great) satisfactions of life. Drifting along is too easy to do." [9]

A Readiness Exercise

Everywhere I go I get the question "how do I know that I am ready for transition?" To help me respond, I developed a short readiness exercise to help women answer this question. The objective of the exercise is to raise your awareness of the assumptions involved in transition. I found that this exercise helped women decide for themselves how to proceed.

People's awareness of or connection to assumptions about transition differs. Some differences may be generational. For example, in my research women who came of age at the peak of the women's movement in the late 1970s seemed to have an ingrained commitment to exploring their identity. It was second nature to them. In comparison, I found that women only ten years younger were completely unfamiliar with that terrain.

The exercise will not give you an answer or tell you emphatically that transitioning is right for you. What it will do is raise your awareness of the issues that stand at the core of the work in transitioning. The decision to proceed is entirely your own.

Take some time to answer the questions in the box. There are no right or wrong answers. Please write down your answers either electronically or by using a pencil and paper. We will return to your answers in later chapters.

Readiness Assessment

1) Introduce yourself two separate times. First, prepare a one-sentence introduction. After that prepare a three- to five-sentence introduction. Imagine you are your audience. Once you are ready, introduce yourself out loud using both the short and long versions. Are there major themes that you emphasized? Highlight them or write them down.

2) Classify the themes from your answer to the question in a) by distributing them into three discrete buckets. Label the buckets with the following titles: Firmly Established, May Need Updating, and Possibly Outgrown or No Longer Relevant. What do you notice about the classification of your themes?

3) Imagine you are being interviewed by your favorite media outlet about your greatest lifetime achievements. What are you discussing with your interviewer? Remember these achievements can be taken from anything that holds meaning for you. Now think through your response a little further by asking yourself these follow-on questions. Is this something you have already achieved? How much of your day-to-day activities are involved in working with this capacity? Do you encounter people or things that limit your ability to interact with or fully realize this capacity?

4) Imagine that you could remove all of the boundaries or limitations that came to mind in response to the last question in c). Now answer the question again. Would you describe your capabilities differently without these limitations or boundaries?

5) Can you talk out loud for one minute about the values you hold most dear? Please get a stop watch and talk for 60 seconds. Once your talk is complete, spend time thinking about what you chose to talk about. Write down headlines for each topic. Classify the headlines into the same buckets that we used in step b) above: Firmly Established, May Need Updating, and Possibly Outgrown or No Longer Relevant.

A woman, Renee, with whom I did this exercise responded to the one-sentence challenge in 1) in the following way: "Honduran single mother of two and professor at Hunter College." Her longer description was "I am a single-parent and a psychology professor at Hunter. I am a first generation American having been born to immigrant parents. My mother was a Seventh Day Adventist who came here as a child. She divorced my dad when I was very young. I have three children living with me, two of my own and a nephew from California. I live in Queens close to my sister and our extended family."

Most of her themes, she was quick to point out, revolved around her connection to the Latin community. This community was very present in her life and represented a big part of her identity. Her identity was also intertwined with the importance of education, a theme first introduced to her by her mother. She looked at it as an important value that she imparted to her children and all those with whom she came in contact. She placed all of her themes in the firmly established bucket. Even more clear to Renee was her love of her work and the values that it represented. She saw enormous potential in her future as a professor and did not view her capacity as limited in any way. She said it would be easier if her kids' dad helped out more. But she did not view this as a gate or an obstacle that was limiting her. Nor did she view her identity or values as mobile or requiring a refresh.

Renee's assessment was markedly different from my own. I arrived at the exercise with a series of questions related to my assumptions about the largely masculine-defined linear career progression that made a large part of my identity. This was coming increasingly in conflict with other components of my identity, like parenting or being active in my community. Both of these I quickly deposited in the Needs Updating bucket. So too my values were influx, not so much my personal values but the value that I had historically put on ascending into higher echelons of corporate hierarchies. My personal calculus about the risk/reward of continuing to progress into higher and higher levels of corporate America was changing radically. Was what I would be asked to give up in corporate America worth the reward I would get there for doing so? Thanks to the assessment, the values about work and financial well-being went into the "Possibly Outgrown or Needs Updating" bucket.

If I exited that world that I knew so well, then what? I would have to rely on transition to help me answer that question.

The Transitioning Process

Transition represents an enormous opportunity for women who choose to initiate it. When faced with the need to change, some choose transition over change. For those who do, the Transitioning Process is a modular, highly structured tool that can assist a woman as she re-examines her assumptions around identity, capacity, or values and uses new building blocks in looking forward to answer the question "what next?" The design emerged out of issues that I encountered repeatedly in my research. It was created based on proven models. It is flexible, ready to accommodate different scopes and pace. While many may wonder if they should or could begin, each individual woman is the only one who can make the ultimate determination. To assist in that decision, there is a short exercise that can provide insight into the nature of the assumptions that lie at the heart of transition. The next two chapters will introduce the steps in each of the phases of the Transitioning Process. The first step, of course, will focus on envisioning our future.

CHAPTER 6

Our First Steps

All of us arrive at transition differently. There are some who arrive at transition able to articulate a future. There are others who arrive at transition aware of a gap between who they have become and the person who they would like to be. Still others—the great majority of women in my research—arrive at transition not knowing what might be next. For these women, intention or instincts or circumstances point them in the direction of transition—direction fraught with uncertainty.

Rita, an experienced trainer, thanks to her decade-long service in the US Coast Guard, talked about her transition's earliest steps. "Where did I go wrong?" she said as she described her thinking at the beginning. She never planned on transition. Every day she stood back to ask herself, "Why is this happening to me?" Rita, who was in her late thirties, talked to me as we sat in a coffee shop outside Washington, DC. "One day my husband, who also served in the military, came home and told me he was in love with another woman. I was devastated. It shattered everything I had ever believed in." Twelve months later, Rita filed to withdraw from military service. "I was scared. I felt like failure. I knew I wanted to be on my own two feet." The biggest challenge? "It was so hard living up to my past self. My past self was awesome."

This chapter introduces Envision, the start of transitioning. The chapter educates women on Envision's four steps. The chapter also explores how much of ourselves we commitment to the transitioning process, our engagement.

Envision

Envision is the four-step initial phase of transitioning. In it, women create a hypothesis about their own future based upon a re-examination of the assumptions at the heart of transition. In this phase a woman develops new thinking about how she will make meaning in her life.

Envision has four sequential steps (see Figure 6.1 Transition Toolkit). They are developing a Fast First Draft; conducting Brainstorming

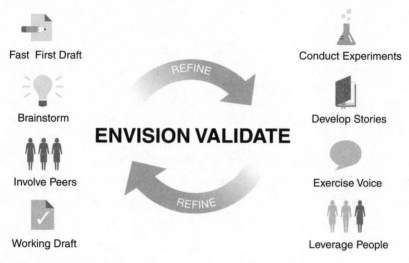

Fast First Draft

Conduct Experiments

Brainstorm

Develop Stories

ENVISION VALIDATE

Involve Peers

Exercise Voice

Working Draft

Leverage People

Figure 6.1   The transition toolkit.

Exercises; engaging Peer Groups; and creating a Working Draft. The first activity requires women to create a baseline response to a set of questions about what their future might look like. Next, women are tasked with broadening their outlook on possible futures by participating in brainstorming exercises meant to be expansive. Once complete, the initial questions are revisited and refined through outreach to Peers and additional individual work. This step-by-step approach is designed to help women work through an abstract and potentially stressful first step—envisioning their own futures.

In Envision, we will not interrogate specific assumptions related to transition's definition, like identity or capacity. Instead, Envision relies on broad questions and activities that require a woman to form an opinion about the core assumptions while executing a task. The Envision toolkit allows for any and all elements of our assumptions to be worked on as we proceed through the transitioning process.

As I mentioned earlier, many women short change Envision, believing that it is too difficult or that their lack of "knowing the answer" about their future is reason enough not to continue. Envision addresses this hesitation by breaking down tasks into manageable steps. Many who use the Transition Toolkit have had experience in career planning, a process that frequently relies on past-focused activities. Envision works hard to leverage past experiences while keeping a forward-looking goal. Addie Swartz,

CEO of reacHIRE,[1] a back-to-work solution for women who voluntarily exit the workforce, made note of the importance of Envision's forward-looking output: "It's not about who they were, it's about who they can be, and how they can morph to get there. It's about possibility and future, not being so focused on what they were in the past—level-wise, salary-wise, or any-other-focus-wise."

Developing a Fast First Draft

Envision's first step is the Fast First Draft. The goal of the Fast First Draft is to develop a baseline of a woman's thinking about her future. Similar to the concept of the "elevator pitch," the Fast First Draft is based on a set of questions that women answer in rapid-fire fashion and as if they have just completed their current transition. This future point in time could be measured in months or even in years, depending on the individual woman's time frame for transition.

The questions as defined in Figure 6.2 help women begin to acknowledge and to link concepts important to them, like values and impact. Some women complete the exercise quickly. Others struggle. It does not matter how completely you answer any of the questions. The work at this stage does not have to be accurate. Your best guesstimate is fine. The goal is to commit something, anything, to writing. We will refine and revise the output of this step in later steps.

One woman, Patricia, whose voice was particularly helpful in designing this exercise, summarized her starting point as "I finally have the time to do something, but I do not know what I want to do." She was the mother of two. Patricia and her husband were both lawyers. She had been out of the workforce for almost a decade.

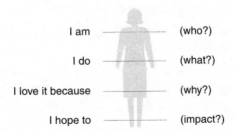

Figure 6.2 Fast first draft.

She held two jobs between law school and the time when she stopped working, one as an associate at a large regional firm, and the other as an attorney at a smaller boutique. She quit her job after having her second child. Her decision to leave the workforce was a complex one. She tried to rationalize many factors: a growing distaste for her current job, her husband's erratic and uncompromising schedule, and the economics of child care given the modest salary she drew at the boutique firm where she worked. She acknowledged that her decision to give up a salary was big. She, like many of us, was aware of the hit to our potential lifetime earnings such a departure from the workforce introduces. Yet while she was aware of this, finances were not the most important factor in her decision.

My sense was that if Patricia had been more juiced about what she was doing, the decision would have been harder to make. Both of her jobs were demanding, but she was well up for the task. The office environments were both highly political. The work interesting, although at times it slipped to marginal at best. Neither experience lived up to the excitement that she had felt while in law school, let alone in comparison to the career she had always dreamed of.

Patricia's absence from the workforce only amplified her growing ambivalence toward the law. "I hate the law. I don't think I wasted my time going to law school," she went on, "but I'm not sure how I'd use my degree today." Her confidence had taken a hit in the years since her departure from the workforce. She had interests, but she had not really come to closure on what might be next. "I don't know what I want to do."

Patricia's Fast First Draft was short. She was not able to answer the first three questions at all. She was able to talk about question four, the impact she hoped to have. She wanted to work in a job that benefited her community. Of this she was certain.

This exercise was difficult for me. I stalled for almost a year when trying to work on the questions. Do not get me wrong. I did not sit in my office that entire time cogitating on the possible answers. I filled my days consulting and networking. I looked for a job. Occasionally I would pick up these questions and give them a try. My responses resembled a to-do list. I did not really answer question one at all. I merged questions two and three into a laundry list of possible jobs or industries where I could work.

- Start an online custom tailoring business targeted at working women, BlackPants.com
- Start a human resources consulting business
- Facilitate programs to support young women's social development
- Start a blog focused on women's development
- Get involved in entrepreneurial or start-up activities

All of the ideas were disjointed. Most reflected various versions of my prior self. There was no glue. Nothing held them together. There was little in terms of impact that I could articulate in a coherent fashion.

I did not make much progress beyond editing the lists until two things happened. First, I was introduced to a framework about engagement that I found helpful. Second, I coupled the Fast First Draft output with brainstorming exercises.

Engaging Ourselves

How much of yourself will you put in play in transition? Odd question, right? Many of us have successfully learned how to compartmentalize our lives. We show up as spouses in some places, business owners and managers in others. We are parents and daughters and neighbors in still others. Sometime we fuse these expressions of ourselves. At other times we do not. Everyone, it seems, has adopted a compartmentalized approach to a greater or lesser extent in their lives. How much of who you are will you put forward for transition? When I experienced my trigger that afternoon on the Thames River, I would have told you that I could not engage myself anymore. I was at the point of sheer exhaustion simply responding to all of the ways that I engaged myself on a daily basis. Transition would teach me to think about this in an entirely new way.

I was tipped off about engagement while facilitating a career event at University of Massachusetts Boston's Emerging Leaders Program. I gave the opening remarks and then facilitated a breakout session. I frequently was asked to do these types of events, thanks to my prior role as EVP of Human Resources and Administration for one of the few Fortune 500 companies headquartered in Massachusetts. In the breakout session I asked participants to work through an exercise with me. The first step required them to write down their career goals using a five-year time horizon. After completing the exercise, we spent time sharing answers with each other. Next, I asked participants to answer the following question: "If you had to work for the rest of your life but could not get paid, what would you do?"

That day no one in attendance had the same answer to question one as they did to question two. Did I mention that all the attendees in my breakout session were women? One woman, Evette, a late thirties mother of a young daughter, shared that she was a manager in the finance department of a local utility. In her five-year view she wanted to become a director in that department. Her response to the second question was markedly different. She loved working with children and had a deep sense of commitment to her community. She wanted to combine her prior experience in finance to create a new community-based start-up targeted at children. She was eloquent and engaging. We met Evette, a richly engaging woman, through her second answer.

There are real reasons why we decide to pursue "finance director" and not "community start-up" leader. Asking yourself the reasons why and thinking through how you could close the potential gaps you uncover between these two answers may be the first questions you need to ask yourself. These questions speak to how much of ourselves we will engage in transition.

The process of engaging ourselves was introduced to me again at an event that I already discussed, the community service day that I attended with my husband. That day, one of the facilitators, a gifted youth minister named Sal Caraviello, shared that he gives teens a gift at the conclusion of an annual high school program that he runs. The gift? A "raw" light switch. By "raw" I mean just picked out of a bin at Home Depot. It is a switch with wires hanging out and all components visible. No packaging. With the switch, Sal tells teens that the decision is theirs: they can either choose to turn it on or leave it off. He reminds teens that they can go through life with their switch off. It is their decision.

Using Sal's imagery, you can go through Envisioning—and your life—perfectly well without ever turning your switch on. You can be successful in this "off" setting. You can achieve many things. You can have a wonderful family. You can meet and exceed expectations at work. But all of this doing and achieving might be a safe distance away from exposing the unique, rich, incredibly valuable *you*. Sheila, a married woman with four adult children, who had just turned 60 when she was interviewed for my research, offered, "Be engaged in a life that has value *for you* because that's *the stuff*. It's the stuff that opens the networks, starts the conversations." More than a quarter century ago, Gail Sheehy, author of the 1974 classic *Passages: Predictable Crises of Adulthood*,[2] was discussing this same theme. She said of transition, "It may mean the giving up of familiar but limiting patterns, safe but unrewarding work, values no longer believed in, relationships that have lost their meaning."[3]

How much of you will you turn on for transition?

Conducting Brainstorming Exercises

Envision's second step is to conduct brainstorming exercises. These exercises help women generate new ideas about their futures. The demands of our daily lives make it difficult to think outside of the box. These exercises are designed to help women do exactly that. What brainstorming exercises will not do is provide you with an answer. Brainstorming may help you think more broadly about your options. If you do that, you may then be able to identify new and potentially important opportunities that had not been previously on your radar screen. It will not be until we revisit the questions contained in the Fast First Draft that anything close to an *answer* might emerge for you.

This section highlights two brainstorming approaches useful in transitioning: a scenario-planning technique and a strengths inventory technique. I recommend that you experiment with both approaches as you work through Envision.

Brainstorming Option #1: Scenario Planning
Scenario Planning is a brainstorming technique that generates ideas based upon the creation of stories about the future. The technique was created in the late 1960s at Royal Dutch Shell to assist managers in making decisions

about investments, the payoffs of which would be many decades into the future.[4] Employees at Royal Dutch Shell created their stories by visiting knowledgeable people and researching all sides of critical issues, even the contrarian views. They then created short narratives to encompass what they learned. These narratives, known as scenarios, were then used as inputs to brainstorming sessions. The technique's reliance on consulting others is common and powerful. Readers familiar with the histories of Microsoft and Apple know that Bill Gates and Steve Jobs did exactly that at the formative stages of their companies. Each man visited Xerox Parc.[5] Royal Dutch Shell credited scenario planning with helping managers "stretch to see what they were not seeing."[6]

Scenario Planning requires you to write a three-to-five-sentence story that describes a future state relevant to you. Since transition is about identity and how we make meaning in our world, women often used external expressions of their transition in creating scenarios. For example, women who were in transition due to retirement, career change, job loss, or the desire to re-engage in the workforce tended to explore scenarios that involved possibilities about work or anticipated changes in one's professional environment. There were others for whom work was outside of their interest. For example, one woman, Katrina, investigated holistic health and lifestyle choices in her scenarios. She described her transition as being triggered by happiness. She had finally concluded a painful divorce. In generating ideas about what scenarios to develop, women often found it useful to consult the readiness exercise conducted at the conclusion of chapter 5.

As I sat down to do my own scenario planning, I had already concluded some important things about my future. I realized that many of the traditional next steps in terms of jobs did not hold meaning for me. I was not interested in doing what I had just done in a bigger company or different industry. This realization took me in another direction. I began by listing themes that could be the focus of a scenario. The best scenarios I wrote involved how I could contribute to shaping broader agendas. This terminology was how I described my interest beyond getting the next job. I am very socially and community minded, so these scenarios interested me. The agendas varied—some were relevant to national or international arenas, and others were more tailored to the community in which I lived.

One reflected back to my Fast First Draft's idea of getting involved in topics related to young girl's social development. They were all over the place. No scenario that I developed was a silver bullet. The scenarios were not the answer. However, they very successfully got me thinking more broadly than my "to-do" list response to the Fast First Draft. As a brainstorming exercise the technique proved useful.

Identifying which scenarios to develop can often be a stumbling block. The box below offers a list of prompts that may help in identifying a scenario or two to start with. I landed on my scenarios by looking at what I was not willing to do: a list of not's. Once I really thought about what was on the list of not's, it allowed me to write down some potential ideas for the future that proved beneficial.

Struggling with scenario topics? Try these prompts.
- A dream job or industry
- A list of activities that make you happy
- A desired future state
- A toast about you to be given at your next milestone birthday
- Output from your readiness assessment
- A list of what you dreamed about as a young child

Pamela, a long-time employee in the financial aid office of a prestigious university, said, "My transition is on the personal side." She had always been the one to raise her hand for more at work. She asked her boss repeatedly, "Have you got anything new?" She had benefited from this attitude in terms of being given more responsibility and opportunity. Even so, she had begun feeling really restless over the past several years. She decided her transition was exploring more about who she was. "I'm a mother. A wife. I am always putting everybody else first. My real transition is related to that. It is so hard putting myself first." Her scenario development consisted of things that she wanted to pursue for herself.

Most scenario development requires research of some kind. The research can be conducted from the quiet confines of your own home. We have the Internet with its multitude of resources—Ted Talks, YouTube videos, professors who teach Massively Open Online Courses, WebEx seminars, or SKYPE calls. You name it. Research in support of developing scenarios can be done on, say, a Tuesday evening from virtually anywhere there is an Internet connection free of censorship. Women found it helpful to plan their research approach, particularly when it involved the Internet. For those women, we wrote out a set of questions for their online work. In this way you can better manage your time. It is often helpful to list the topics you will explore, the people or points of view that you want to investigate, or even how to identify whose views may be contrary to yours.

Meredith was surprised because she used scenario planning to iden-tify a new professional path, but discovered that she found out important information about values and what was driving her decision. She special-ized in scientific marketing at a prestigious biotech company. She had a degree in biology and an MBA. Shortly after having a child, she was recruited away from the biotech company to join a technology start-up. This career move allowed her to reposition her analytical and writing skills at a smaller company. At the company, she wrote technical papers aimed at scientific customers and did other analytically intensive projects. After a few years, Meredith wanted to return to the world from which she had come, product-driven biotech marketing.

Unfortunately, Meredith's skills were now viewed as dated by recruiters for the large biotech firms. She found this incredibly frustrating and sad. "How can they question my skills?" she said, heartbroken. She continued to look for jobs at the big biotechs, but was also considering some broader issues related to transition. She liked the scenario-planning approach. She listened to Ted Talks and conducted research on the future of techni-cal and scientific writing. She loved learning about how big data would influence drug development and the scientific evidence she relied upon in her writing. She attended a few online teleconferences. She wrote down a bulleted list of trends that might impact the field. With this scenario she brainstormed a list of new potential targets for her job search. What this exercise also did was to alert her to other factors present in her choices. The prestige and earnings capabilities from her prior jobs were important parts of her identity. She liked the instant credibility they created for her at work as well as in social circles. She wondered how she might feel if she chose to move in another direction.

Meredith's transition began as a job search. As she got further and further into it, she realized that many of her assumptions were at play in determining which job or industries were viable. Meredith kept two tracks going in her pursuits: a job search targeted at biotech firms, and a slowly emerging commitment to transition. Brainstorming helped her engage more actively with the latter.

Brainstorming Option #2: Strengths Inventory

The other brainstorming technique is a three-step Skills Inventory that I created after working with women through transition. The objective of the exercise is to help women identify and acknowledge that their strengths may express themselves in new ways in transition. In the exercise, women create an inventory of strengths, classify the strengths according to their prominence, and then work to assemble the strengths into meaningful new combinations. The exercise asks you to think broadly about skills, particularly those skills that may be present but are not utilized in paid work.

The first step in the technique asks you to inventory your strengths. Some people struggle with this request, as if saying, "What strengths?" You are not alone if you find yourself in this category. A neighbor of mine, Kathleen, shared a story that might offer some perspective on this. Kathleen volunteered for years at a State University of New York women's transition center. One of the center's most popular programs was a semi-nar for career changers. The seminar had an application and acceptance process. The application process required women to articulate their skills and achievements. Kathleen shared with me that many women arrived at the application process flummoxed, as if saying, "What skills?"

"The group that always surprised us were the teachers," Kathleen said. "They struggled the most. They did not recognize that their role as teach-ers translated into planning and organizational skills; public speaking skills; and conflict resolution skills." I found Kathleen's story provoca-tive in that it highlights the challenges in thinking objectively about the strengths that we demonstrate every day.

Can you isolate those things about you that are your strengths regard-less of whether someone else identifies them as such? Consider all of your roles, not just those contained in your last formal job review or for which you are paid. The inventory will be incomplete if it is a reiteration of someone else's opinion of you. Be aware that many of us may start with strengths for which we have been rewarded. Are these in fact valid or complete? Gail Rentsch, author of *Smart Women Don't Retire—They Break Free,* said, "How do you sort out those things that are truly important, that make you tick, from those things you learned to consider important only because you got approval or rewards for them?"[7] Her comment deserves serious consideration.

If you are struggling with this inventory, write down what you do on a weekly or monthly basis. From there imagine that you need to interview and hire someone to execute all of those roles. What strengths will you screen for as you interview the perfect candidate? That list can serve as a catalyst to your thinking about your own unique strengths.

The next step asks you to classify your strengths into categories by prominence: high, medium, or low. The classification is based on how these strengths are present for you today. I find it easiest to visualize this sorting exercise. I created one for myself using coin-sized circles. The strengths that are prominent are quarter sized, and those less so are dime sized.

An excerpt from my classified strengths inventory is presented as Figure 6.3. A large circle of mine was engaging people. I love it, from initiating small teams at work to inviting neighbors over for a cooking soirée the Wednesday evening before Thanksgiving. I do it effortlessly and continuously. On the opposite side of my classification were skills that are present for me but infrequently used. These little bubbles included public speaking, social justice work or structuring arguments, each of which I

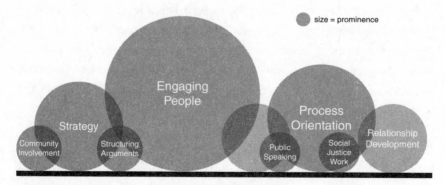

Figure 6.3 Excerpt of author's strengths by prominence.

love but do less often. In doing the exercise, I relied on input that I had gathered from prior situations, like feedback from a colleague with whom I worked on the Board of Directors at my prior employer. "You are the best I've ever seen at framing discussions," he offered.

The final step involves the brainstorming part of the exercise: reassembling strengths into new combinations. If you are having difficulty with this, think about it as similar to anagrams. An anagram is a word puzzle that rearranges the letters of original words into new words,[8] like "silent" and "listen." Same letters but two different words. In working with strengths, women assemble interesting "what if" combinations. For me this led to "what if I combined my love of people with my ability to structure arguments?" This technique also underscores an important observation that I made in working with women on transition. Transition rarely expressed itself as a sudden departure from a prior self. Instead, transition tended to more commonly be a recombination of elements of oneself, some of which may have been previously de-emphasized. Brenda, the thirty-five-year-old married woman with no children, said when thinking through this exercise, "I feel like I'm beginning to discover talents that were misaligned, misappropriated."

Brainstorming techniques in transition are structured to assist us at being expansive. Neither exercise will provide you an answer or give you a hypothesis about your future. It should, however, provide a basis for broader exploration of what will hold meaning for you as you continue through the last two steps.

Engaging Our Peers

Envision's third step involves establishing a Peer Group to support your exploration. This group will be asked to provide objective, unbiased feedback and serve as a sounding board for you as you talk out loud about what might be ahead. This support group will serve as an invaluable source of affirmation, a critical success factor to women transitioning that we heard about in chapter 4. Gloria Steinem referred to support groups in the following manner at a recent event sponsored by The Commonwealth Institute:[9] "We called them consciousness raising groups, you call them book groups." By whatever vocabulary, this group will serve an invaluable function in your transitioning work.

What is a Peer Group? It is two to six people whom you recruit to support your transitioning process. Peer Group's participants can be anyone you would like who can listen objectively and ask good questions. At times they will need to push back on you or take a different—potentially unpopular—position. Therefore, identifying people whom you trust is important. The Peers can meet all at once or individually with you. I met with members of my peer group individually because time constraints precluded group meetings. The one downside? It required more work on my part because I was constantly updating the others on conversations with the rest of the members.

There are those who may not be great choices as participants. Best friends, mothers, and husbands may be in this category. Why? Those closest to us may introduce biases that direct us away from the very conversations we should be having with our Peers. Many my research study noted that the best advice comes from those who are new or relatively new to us. Members of your Peer Group should listen without any preconceived notions about who or what we are. One woman, Shauna, a retired technology manager and mother of three, described why her husband of 40 years could not serve in her Peer Group. "Very often what comes through is his need for me. He is too involved with me as his wife. If I did something weird, that would probably affect him."

Identifying Peers outside of our closest existing ties may reduce the risk to your process that these biases represent. INSEAD Professor Herminia Ibarra in her book, *Working Identity*,[10] found that close ties bring inherent biases that can impede our ability to reassess and explore new options. "We need to realize that our intimates – spouses, bosses, close friends, parents – expect us to remain the same, and they may pressure us to be consistent."[11] These biases can be damaging and difficult to recognize. Sheila, a Texan who helped me test Envision's steps, was no stranger to transition. She had an effervescent and instantly engaging personality. It seemed as if anyone meeting her would think that they had known her for a long time. In a period of ten years, Sheila had gotten married, started a family, and changed careers. She was not finished. Her dream was to create a new business that could combine her love of the sales process with her desire to parent in a way that was comfortable for her. She wanted to start a consulting business that would help companies with their sales processes. She had an elementary school-aged son. Even though she had spent a lot of time working on her ideas and exploring ways to start the business, she recalled the perspective of those around her, including her husband and her in-laws. They were quick to tamp down her dreams, as if to say, "*Be realistic.*"

In sharing information about their Peers, women sought new, more objective relationships. Beverly, a woman who chose transition after retirement, said, "I think people who have been through it before and for me sometimes it's people who are actually new to me."

The Peer Group will act in a variety of ways. They will react to your hypothesis. They will challenge your assumptions by asking questions. They will help you identify new avenues to explore based upon your initial work. Your role in the group is one of facilitator and narrator. Claire, an early forties single mother of a college student, remarked that her Peer Group helped her listen more carefully to her instincts. "The only thing I would say is that almost every single person in my life told me that I was making the wrong decision, including my boyfriend, who is one of the most supportive people in my life." Claire viewed her decision to transition as an opportunity, even though those around her were saying, "Don't quit your job until you know what you plan to do." She was grateful to three people who served in her Peer Group. "I was so sure about what I needed. Their support was really empowering. Transition is really not about where other people are, but really having an understanding of where you are yourself. I have not looked back once."

Schedule your first meeting after recruiting a few members to serve. The inset box lists a starting agenda. The agenda's content can be spread over multiple meetings.

My Peer Group was broad and included a man who was its most vocal and engaged member. The one amazing gift that my Peer Group gave me was their presumption of my success. They were not privy to the negative self-talk that accompanied the earliest stages of my transition. From their perspective, there was no question about my ability to succeed in anything I chose to focus on. This alone was an important lesson to me. It recharged me. It helped me look beyond some false conclusions that had become a part of my internal talk track. Their simple gift helped me keep going.

Engaging Our Peer Group: Sample Agenda

- Introduction Icebreaker
  - Ask everyone to introduce the person on their left.
  - Ask everyone to describe a transition they have made.
- Describe why you chose transition.
- Describe what you hope to gain in transitioning.
- Share your output from your Fast First Draft or your Working Draft* with the group.
- Ask peers to share one thing they liked about draft.
- Ask peers to share one thing they wished were different about your draft.
- Ask peers to list questions that they hope you will explore before finalizing your draft.
- Share with the group the areas with which you are most comfortable and least comfortable in your draft.
- Talk with your peers about your next steps. Make sure you get the group's input regarding your priorities.
  - * Output from Envisioning's final step

Peer Groups meet regularly, although not often. Their members may need to be available to you by phone or by other means as you work through the various steps in the process. The Peer Group continues its support as you move through Validate and assess whether or not you will refine your thinking.

Creating A Working Draft

Envision's last step is the Working Draft. The Working Draft is a revision of your Fast First Draft that is informed by the other Envision steps. It reflects the work that you have done to re-examine the assumptions that lie at the heart of transition—identity, capacity, and values. It uses the same questionnaire that you used in the Fast First Draft (Figure 6.1), only this time your output has the benefit of your thinking and output from the intervening steps. Meredith, the biotech expert mentioned above, asked me an important question as we worked through this exercise: "Do you have to create a different person or a different version?" She came from an environment in which the term "versions" stood for important new features or upgrades to previously released products. I loved her vocabulary. *Versions*.

Please take a moment to again write out the answers to the four questions (see Figure 6.2). With your revised responses, review the answers next to the output of your Readiness Exercise from chapter 5. Do you notice anything about your responses to Envision's fourth step?

I found that it was helpful to electronically write out the answers daily over one week's time. During the first three or four days, I saw a large change day-to-day in my responses. By doing this day over day, I began to question the limits that I still had established in my mind. It was as if each day I kept asking myself, "Why not more?" I finally landed on a Working Draft that included "be a recognized thought leader on women's development issues." This output was astonishing. It was expansive, and engaging and surprisingly well aligned with who I was. It was still characterized by uncertainty. What, after all, did it mean?

Envision allowed me to travel from considering a new start-up focused on historical although limited experiences with SEC compliant processes to considering something that was deeply meaningful to me. Only me. In theory it incorporated many of my strengths—some of which I had overlooked for many years. I was surprised by this tack and even more surprised by how it made me smile.

Envision

Transition requires us to re-examine our assumptions about identity, capacity, and or values. Envision is the first phase of the process that supports our work in re-examining these assumptions. It is tailored to the internal, highly personal issues that influence how we make meaning in our lives. Envision uses a practical step-by-step approach to help us think through our future. Our *own* futures. The output of this phase is a ready-to-be-tested hypothesis, not an answer. Ideally, the hypothesis can engage the fullness of who we are. Our next phase will focus on testing and refining this output into something realizable.

CHAPTER 7

Reaching Forward

With my Working Draft in hand, I was ready to continue. But with what? My output from Envision, while incredibly interesting, was a little vague. It was not really actionable. After all, I was not sure what it meant to pursue my interests in women's development or for that matter how I would integrate my professional experience. I needed to find a way to advance my thinking in and around all of the other demands of my life. It was too exciting to ignore, but it was not entirely clear to me how to proceed. Thanks to the voices of the women in my research, I had a few ideas.

Stephanie, a mother of three who had just turned 40, intentionally chose transition. Her decision did not eliminate the very real doubts and uncertainty she felt, however. She was scared. Her trigger was a complex set of decisions that she and her husband made. Both had demanding careers in the Los Angeles area. She had worked for 17 years in talent management. Her husband had worked in the film industry. They moved to Oregon when their eldest son was entering kindergarten and their twin sons were 18 months old. It was the first move Stephanie had ever made that was not driven by her career. Her eldest was entering kindergarten with an IEP, an individualized education plan, due to a recent diagnosis of a learning disability.

Upon arrival in Oregon, Stephanie acclimated her family to their new community. "I didn't know anything about transition when we packed up and headed north. I didn't know what I was searching for." She explored and tested new activities once she got everyone settled. She volunteered and searched for part-time work. "My experience in LA helped. There I was always getting new responsibilities or new promotions every year or two. That perspective helped."

"The defining moment," she said, "didn't come until my twins were heading off to kindergarten." That was the time to act on what she had learned about herself. "I decided to take advantage of things that fueled me, that I learned about since our move to Oregon." Stephanie got a job with responsibility for talent at a local company, thanks to a conversation with another parent at the school her children attended. While the job itself was a victory, Stephanie credited her transition with more than just a new paycheck. "I'm surprised by how much I've changed. I never realized what this was all about. In a weird way transition helped me reclaim me. But I also learned things I never knew about myself."

I heard the experimentation voiced by Stephanie repeatedly as I talked with other women. This approach was very familiar to me, because of my background as an entrepreneur. I realized that I had already adopted it in part as I continued my own transition work.

This chapter introduces Validate, the Transitioning Process's second phase, which helps us test and improve upon the work of Envision. The chapter also presents its four tools: conducting experiments, developing stories, exercising voice, and leveraging people. Together, these tools support women through this exciting and empowering stage of transitioning.

Validate

Validate is a process designed to help us test and refine our Working Draft. The process acts as a toolkit, offering four options for women to deploy in a self-paced fashion. The tools are conducting experiments, developing stories, exercising our voice, and leveraging people (see Figure 7.1). Most women use the tools repeatedly over a period of time. The phase will differ

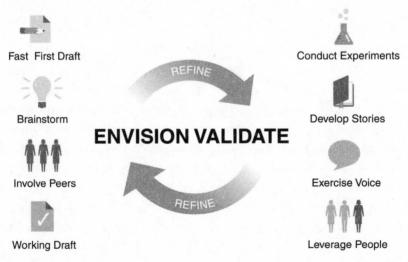

Figure 7.1 The transition toolkit.

from individual to individual because women can customize the use of the tools to fit their validation needs. You may choose to execute a series of experiments. Your neighbor may choose to work on developing her story and then leveraging other people to test it out.

The goal of Validate is to generate new information that you can then use to assess your Working Draft: how resilient, valid, strong, accurate, and solid are your assumptions and conclusions? Women make slight refinements in their Working Draft as they iterate through the use of Validate's tools. Each of the iterations generates learning. Following these steps, women often need to cycle back to Envision and refine their entire Working Draft. This loop back is part of the process of transition: it does not mean that the original Envision Phase and Working Draft were inadequate or wrong. It represents another opportunity to reimagine the "possible."

Conducting Experiments

Experiments are tests or trials tailored to meet a learning objective that is focused on your Working Draft. I found it best to state the learning objective explicitly, as in, "What I am trying to understand from the test?" This section will talk about the types of experiments we may employ during validation and the pitfalls to be aware of in getting ready for them.

Experiments can take many forms. A new job. A volunteer opportunity. A trial period. A networking meeting. A walk with a friend. A research endeavor. Enrollment in a course. A revised schedule. There is not one "right" model. We can design experiments to be less weighty than the entirety of our transition. They can be directed by our curiosities or even our playfulness, two traits that we do not often consider as we stare down uncertainty. Experiments allow us to try new things without making a life-altering commitment. This helps us reduce risk in transition. Experiments help us avoid major commitments right out of the box. Instead, major commitments are reserved for those times after we have gathered pertinent information and refined and validated our Working Draft.

Experiments, particularly the early ones, can allow us to continue our other activities while exploring transition. One woman, Freda, from San Francisco, talked about the difficult toggle between working on transition while working full time and parenting. Freda was in her early forties and had recently switched jobs. In the prior five years, she had gotten married and had twins. She took a job that was not her dream job after thinking carefully about identity and what the future needed to be for her. Of her current state, she said, "I'm still doing it. I'm actually thinking about what's next."

Freda did not have the luxury of not working full time while she experimented. Instead she had decided to work differently, given what she described as an ongoing transition. "I've been trying to craft my thinking about what it is that I want to do as my own independent entity. I think I want to be a project management consultant." She was happy that she had been able to articulate a Working Draft, which in its fullness also alluded to her updated values and purpose. "So I'm doing it, experimenting, that is. I took a workshop on project management tools and apps. At work I'm choosing what to get involved in. I've put my hand up to help on a project that is just getting underway. We plan to evaluate the company's entire project portfolio. I am exposing myself to tools and people. I'm getting my job done, but I'm also thinking about myself." She put her transition process on a multiyear pace due to real constraints introduced by her children and family.

"Right now, this works for me and I have lots of flexibility. You can probably do a good job and make your money, but if you are in transition you have to rethink your identity and how you think about your job. You have to find space to explore other things. There is a trick to it. You have to work out managing your reality and managing your dream. How do you nurture your dream and survive?"

Conducting workplace-based experiments is being supported more and more today, thanks to emerging trends in the workplace. The emergence of the "GIG economy" is one example. This trend allows employees to parachute into and out of project-based work more easily. A "gig" is a term used to represent event- or project-driven employment typically performed by individuals serving as independent contractors instead of as full-time employees. Many business leaders tie its emergence to the decline of the traditional lifelong career model. Tina Brown, founder of *The Daily Beast* and former editor of *Vanity Fair* and *The New Yorker*, talked recently about this trend with students at Babson College's Olin School of Management. "No one I know has a job anymore; everyone has gigs."[1] Another growing trend is the prevalence of adult internships. Historically the domain of high school and college-aged students, internships offer valuable insight into a new environment. Carol Fishman Cohen, coauthor of *Back on the Career Track* and cofounder of iRelaunch, a comprehensive career re-entry resource, identified this trend as critical to those women who return to work after a prolonged absence. "It is ideal for women to have a current project that gives them experience in their targeted industry," said Ms. Cohen.[2] While still not commonplace, these trends positively support the work of experimentation.

Many women ask me about the usefulness of psychological testing as a form of experimentation. My answer is "yes, these types of tests and assessments can be used as a means of further validating your Working Draft." What they cannot do, however, is answer the question "what's next for me?" For those unfamiliar with psychological testing, it focuses on personal behaviors thought to measure an attribute or predict an outcome. This type of testing typically requires a financial investment and is usually administered by a third-party expert. Many women have experienced psychological testing either through career planning activities on college campuses or through employer-sponsored professional development programs. Psychological testing can take many forms, including personality, intelligence, motivation, mechanical ability, vocational preference, and special abilities tests.[3] Names like the Myer Briggs Type Indicator or the Hogan Motives, Values and Preferences Inventory may be familiar to you. While these tests can be useful in validating the soundness of your Working Draft, they rarely provide you with an answer about your future, as women who undertake such testing often hope for.

In crafting your experiments, be on the lookout for desired outcomes that are overly narrow or simplistic. In the face of uncertainty, we often set up simple "yes or no" alternatives as a means of managing risk. While useful, this approach can limit the value of experimentation. A longtime colleague of mine, Beth, who lives in Southern California, called one day to ask my advice. She was in the midst of a transition. Beth is a recently divorced single mom of a three teenage girls. She had just recovered from a scary cardiac health issue. "Can you help me get an interview?" she asked. Her target was a prestigious lab that served as an external research and development (R&D) department for larger, more established companies.

Beth had opted for a severance package in a reorganization at her prior employer. Even though the package was attractive, Beth did not have the luxury of staying out of work very long.

"I really want to work for them," she started out saying. She was a marketing guru who hoped that her skills could be quickly redeployed in a new industry. I was fascinated by the urgent binary decision she had created. It was this company or no company in that industry. I was floored. "Why not some other companies, too, if this one is so interesting?" I asked. But it was this boutique or nothing. She had done some research. No other firm seemed of the caliber of her target in terms of prestige and quality of the projects that they took on.

Had her call come prior to my transition, I probably would have rolled up my sleeves to help her get an interview. Instead, I simply asked a question. "How do you know that this company is it?" I asked. My question got her talking. Almost in passing she mentioned that there was another, larger lab that offered a training program for career changers. She did not want anything to do with them. They were not prestigious enough. I shared with her my growing belief in the usefulness of experiments, particularly in light of the massive changes she was contemplating. By my logic, she should more carefully consider the company with the training program. It could be her petri dish, not her destination but a stepping-stone designed to further her understanding of the scientific community and of herself as she waded further and further into a new identity.

Experiments are invaluable to transition because they help us ascertain the correctness of our hypothesis, and they invariably introduce us to new thinking. One of my experiments in women's development was starting a blog, Novofemina.com. My learning objective was to explore whether or not there was any depth to the issue of women's transition, a subject that captivated my imagination. Within a few months of weekly posts my learning objective had been met. Not only had I validated my own interest in the topic but I also learned additional information that was previously unknown to me. The experiment took a couple of hours a week. The experiment convinced me to continue exploring the topic and to refine my overall Working Draft. This refinement step is responsible for the broadening of my research that stands as the backbone to this book. My Peer Group was also involved as I thought through how to respond to the learning that emerged from my experiment. In the words of one of my

Peer Group's members after he saw the early posts and traffic statistics on the site, "You need to *dream bigger.*"

Developing Stories

The next tool in Validate's toolkit is Developing Stories. A story illustrates the unique value you bring to a situation. Stories are fundamental to transition. They serve as the currency through which others listen as we realign elements of ourselves. Stories also operate as an important platform on which we test our desired future state with others. Whether your story hails from volunteering, childrearing, or divesting a corporate division, it is worth telling if it is in your own voice and meaningfully conveys who you are.

Our Working Draft stands at the center of our story development in transition. With stories we can test and retest it. Through stories we gain important information from how our audience responds to the story and what questions it prompts them to ask. Early in my transition, I used a vague reference to my status as my story's central feature. "I am on sabbatical" was the start of my story. This turned out to be a disaster because it invariably led people to assume that I was a tenured professor. Once I completed Envision, I replaced the vague references with a short story about my interest in women's development. Even though I was still unclear what it meant, I was astonished by the reaction that I got from listeners. People brightened. They asked questions. The story became a means through which I expanded the questions that I was willing to ask myself.

Our story development in transition needs to focus on value instead of relying on a time-based chronology. Chronology is a popular organizing feature in our stories. Bringing awareness to this shift is an important step. Many women with whom I worked, struggled to reframe stories in this way.

"What am I doing wrong?" fumed Leslie, a Florida native. She was trying to secure a new job after close to a decade of interrupted employment due to her children's needs and her own personal health issues. She was a breast cancer survivor. She approached transition with resignation after trying unsuccessfully to replicate the person she had been pre-children and pre-illness. Every element of Leslie's identity was at play in her transition: her health, her finances, her marriage, and her spirituality. She needed a job, she reasoned, as a grounding mechanism while so much else was in flux.

Leslie had extensive professional experience from years working in technology before she started a family. Names like IBM, Oracle, and Akamai were on her resume. This helped her secure many interviews. But she rarely moved on after an initial discussion or two. She was furious when she called that morning. It had happened again. Another prospective employer decided that she was not a fit.

As she and I talked, it was immediately clear to me that she had focused on chronology, not value during her interviews. Her story highlighted her consecutive account leadership roles at one technology leader after another. This approach led her listeners to conclude that she had had a discontinuous work history. Her story did not focus on the client relationships that she secured nor the value that she had contributed at several employers. Leslie felt stuck in crafting her new story because she was not yet able to articulate how all the pieces fit together. She fell back on chronology in situations like many of us when we feel unsure.

Like Leslie, many of us experience interruptions or breaks in our personal narratives that feel destabilizing. Ely, a brand-marketing guru who retired in her late sixties, struggled with this break. "The day before I retired, I was an executive director. I had instant credibility when I walked into a room." She felt as though her skills were all still intact even though her identity as an executive director and expert had been removed. Or had it? She was struggling to establish stories. Internally, she was trying to make sense of her transition, "If I am no longer all of those things, who am I?" On another level, she found her story break difficult because it precluded her from engaging others in her exploration. Barbara Kivowitz,[4] psychologist, author, and expert on transitions in illness, said, "When a narrative doesn't have consistency, or it is broken, we cannot tolerate that, so we make up the pieces that are missing. Very often the pieces that we make up are ones that include self-doubt or self-negative judgments." Kivowitz is a strong believer in the value of stories. "Stories are generative. It is like building an internal construct that makes the transition ok for yourself first before you can communicate it to the outside world."

Stories can be easily crafted and tested. They can be updated as your transition evolves. For those struggling to get started, the story prompts in the inset box may help. Each question is designed to help you draft a new narrative.

> Developing Stories:
> - Using your Working Draft, respond to the following questions:
>   - *What do you want your listener to learn about you?*
>   - *Why does this make sense for you?*
>   - *What value do you alone bring?*
>   - *Why does this have meaning for you?*

A final pitfall to be aware of in developing stories is our potential reliance on others to "fill in the blanks" for us. In transition, our goal is to test *our own* Working Draft not someone else's view of what it should be. We would ask, "I'd like your reaction to _____" instead of "What do you think I should do?" Two very different questions. By losing focus on our Working Draft, we can ask others to fill in the narrative gaps for us instead of providing feedback on our thinking. Phoebe Grace had just completed a master's in social work after leaving the navy. Despite more than ten years of service, she decided to retire because her active duty was increasingly in conflict with her responsibilities as an only child of two parents who were in poor health. After finishing her degree, she struggled to establish an identity outside of the military. She missed the instant credibility that her prior military rank afforded her. So, too, she struggled with her new financial reality since the jobs she had been offered since graduating, while attractive, were at salaries substantially less than what she had been making prior to leaving the military.

Many veterans and others were eager to help her find a new job. When we spoke, she was frustrated because these meet-and-greets were not progressing beyond an initial meeting. "Everyone is always enthusiastic," she shared. "Translating my experience is what is difficult. I was a leader. I've managed through incredibly difficult situations including making split-second life or death decisions." Her narrative focused almost entirely on the chronology of her experiences, a chronology that ended with a question, "What do you think I should do?"

In transition, we need to position those introductory meetings as a means of testing our hypothesis. Phoebe Grace's unsettled state left her clinging to her comfortable chronology and its old familiarity. In networking discussions, her chronology of titles and rank often overshadowed her new desire to discuss how she might add value to complex organizational behavior roles that she sought. Too often, she never got to that statement—time always ran out.

Stories help us craft invaluable bridges to our updated selves in transition. They rely on our Working Drafts and generate valuable feedback. We need to focus on value and avoid letting others write our narrative for us.

Exercising Your Voice

Exercising Your Voice is the quiver in the Validation toolkit. Voice is the oral representation of that which is meaningful to you. It is as critically important in transition as it is throughout a woman's life. Voice is dependent upon the other tools in Validate. In fact, it probably is not fair for me to single it out. How can you tell a story, after all, without voice? If you will permit me, voice is so fundamental to transition that I felt the need to isolate it. This section explores voice, the factors that influence it, and the usefulness of exercising it even in small ways. As we will learn, voice's volume and impact grow with exercise.

Voice is an abstract concept that is sometimes easier to understand from its absence that from its presence. After all, you can talk all day and not say a word about what is important to you or what you believe in. I remember talking with one of my brothers-in-law at a holiday party about two years into my transition. We were huddled in a corner away from the fray. My husband's family is large, so a corner perch is not all that odd for those who want to have a conversation. He looked puzzled as I asked him a question about health care. I was interested in his perspective because I was dealing with a related issue as a member of the Board of Trustees for a $1.5 billion health-care organization in Boston. He is in charge of all ambulatory care at a large public hospital in Queens, New York. To give you a sense of his job, he handles everything from well-baby checkups to oncology in a multicultural, inner-city hospital. His teams rely on translators in over 100 languages. I was sure he would have a perspective on the topic.

After listening to me for a while with a puzzled look on his face, he said, "I thought you were taking it easy." There it was. In an instant I learned how my husband's family characterized my transition. *Taking it easy*. In that moment I was both fascinated by and furious about his remark. Later—in a more composed moment—I realized that this exchange taught me a solid lesson about voice. In the absence of voice, people draw their own conclusions. It does not matter how close you are to these folks. Proximity and relationships are irrelevant. Voice is what matters. My silence or lack of voicing what was up with me, led everyone to reach their own conclusion.

Voice is a mix of what we present to others orally and what others perceive as we present it. Jane was a mid-fifties software developer and a first-generation Asian American. She said of voice, "I think it has a lot to do with how other people perceive us." Jane shared stories of false conclusions that others reached about her simply because of linkages between her voice and her cultural background. She was motivated by voice as a Validation tool because she believed that the message that others took in about her was wrong.

"Because I am silent in, let's say, a conversation, people believe that I have no opinion. I'm silent not because I'm being polite or not because I was taught that way. Until I'm asked I don't respond. That is my style. When I'm asked, I will speak my opinion. When they ask, I give the most-smart opinion. Problem-solving skills." As I listened, there was never any question in her mind that her answers were of high value to her listeners. She concluded with, "The perceived message is very difficult to change." She was no stranger to the conundrum of voice and the perceptions that accompany its presence or absence.

While voice consists of the content of what we say and what others perceive us to have said, its strength and clarity can be influenced by many other factors, like focusing on what others think. Sophia, a woman in her early forties, offered an honest perspective on voice. She cited her transition's trigger as a growing realization of a gap between the expectations of others and what she really wanted. Her career was very important to her.

She derived a large part of her identity from it. She said, "So when you're constantly worrying about what other people think, you lose your voice." She was one of the few in my test group who immediately linked Voice to other elements of our existence, like exhaustion. "I feel like I'm most creative and most authentic when I've slept. When I feel like I've had a little time to myself and I feel like I've got myself back.

"By meeting my husband's needs, my job's needs, my children's needs, I lose myself. I'm exhausted. I'm emotionally drained. So my voice gets lost, because what do I truly want? What is going to make me truly happy? Well, I can't even think about that because I've got a thousand things to do. I guess what I'm saying is that it is hard to hear your voice and your authenticity and your confidence when you feel tired."

Voice can be used as an important validation tool in support of a wide variety of experiments. A career finance professional and mother of two, Blanche offered the most outstanding example of combining voice and experimentation. She had had a series of jobs as she progressed through the finance hierarchy at the company where she worked. About a year prior to her leaving her job, she got the chance to work on a project outside of finance. It was a leadership development initiative targeted at the company's primary lines of business. It captivated her. The experience served as a trigger for her to rethink a whole set of assumptions about work and life. About the same time, she had some personal health issues that played into a wake-up call to explore opportunities outside of the finance department's grueling schedule. She summarized her trigger in the following way, "How am I going to spend my time for the next 20 or so years?"

Blanche was practical. She wanted to find a contract leadership development position that would offer her part-time employment but still allow her to work in this area of newfound interest. How would she make the switch? She decided to experiment prior to making any switch. She wrote down her observations on leadership development in a short presentation. She then networked to gain access to new people. Her outreach went something like, "I'm developing thoughts on leadership development in large corporations. Would you be willing to provide me some feedback?" Her request differed markedly from Phoebe Grace's. For Blanche, networking got her the meetings. Her growing voice gave her the currency to make those meetings matter.

Voice is a fundamental contributor to our ability to move forward in transition. It is a mix of what we present orally and what others perceive in us. Its absence can have a surprisingly negative impact. Coupled with experiments, voice plays a leading role in our self redefinition underway in transition.

Leverage People

Validate's final tool is Leveraging People. Our objective in Leveraging People is to engage others to help us validate our Working Draft. This engagement can take many forms. These people can listen as we talk out loud about our hypothesis. They can sponsor an experiment and provide us feedback. They can help us connect with others. They can listen to our stories and ask questions. They can provide expert advice on a new direction we are considering. I like to think of the folks who serve in this capacity as my external R&D departments. This section will explore exactly what this step entails and discuss the different roles people take on in Leveraging People.

Women often think of this step as networking, with a slightly different objective. Networking typically means meeting with other people to exchange information or make a connection.[5] That characterization is largely correct, although in transition we set a different broader learning objective. In transition we may be leveraging a contact to help us conduct a lengthy experiment. People need to be informed about our Working Draft and their role in helping us with it.

Leveraging People and Engaging Peers are both different and similar. In Leveraging People, the outreach is event driven, whereas we establish an ongoing relationship with our Peer Group in Envision. In Validate, we may reach out to a colleague to help us understand a new industry or what it is like to be a single parent. In Envision, we rely on our peers to have an ongoing conversation with us about our process and the creation of our Working Draft. The two are also similar in that anyone can serve as a member of either group. No specialized experience is required in either. Both groups can bring valuable new connections to your work. I remember one Focus Group attendee, Eleanor, who wanted to turn her attention to studio art after years of working in education. She shared, "I have the wrong reference points for what I want to be doing." She needed to work with her Peer Group and those with whom she interacted in Validate to help her with introductions. The same was true for me. Despite a sizable network developed over my 25-year career, few of my contacts had any depth in women's development. William Bridges, author of *Transitions: Making Sense of Life's Changes*, noted, "In transition we break our connection with how we've come to know ourselves." [6]

The ways you engage other people will differ depending upon the scope and specifics of your Working Draft. But regardless of the specifics, be prepared! Your preparation for these activities will determine the value you get in return. The box below can help you prepare.

Validation's Preparation Basics

- What is your objective for your contact or meeting?
- Have you communicated your objective in advance to the person with whom you are meeting?
- If the event is tremendously successful, what will you have achieved?
- What will this event allow you to do next?
- Are there follow-up activities that you hope to gain agreement on?
- Is there any future involvement or support that you hope to gain agreement on from this individual or event?

Leveraging People is not asking for a job. It is asking people to listen and respond to your evolving Working Draft. It may generate information that will allow you to determine whether and how to proceed. While transition can be a vulnerable time, this step allows you to gain valuable insight from others, all of which is designed to advance your thinking.

Listening in Validation

Validation is tough terrain. It asks us to make public our incomplete very personal work. It asks us to test and retest our ideas. We can feel like a "failure" as we iterate again and again. One of the biggest challenges to the success of Validation is our ability to listen effectively to the information we derive from the use of the tools. This section introduces you to a few reminders to be aware of as you prepare to listen

There are pitfalls to be aware of when we listen during vulnerable times. Transition requires us to validate *our own* thinking, not adopt someone else's. In periods of uncertainty, this can be more difficult than it sounds. One retired executive, Francine, who helped me early in my research process, shared her viewpoint on this. Thanks to a successful career in financial services, Francine serves as a mentor and adviser to many women. Of her mentees she said, "Women will come back and say, 'Well, I talked with so and so. He says that I should do X.'" Francine was distraught over the frequency with which she heard this remark. She went on, "And I say, "That's interesting. 'What do *you* think?'" Francine observed women's propensity to "go do" whatever others direct them to do, as in, "XX thinks I should do Y." She stressed that interpreting the feedback that we hear is just as important as getting the feedback itself. She said of her response to women in this instance, "You have evidence. Instincts. Use them!"

In preparing to use Validate's tools, please remember that you need to stay grounded on your ideas—as expressed in your Working Draft or revisions to it. Even if other people do not get your ideas, it does not mean that your hypothesis is wrong.

Validation can be very stressful, particularly when we hear negative feedback from others. Some women confided that they found themselves getting pushed off-track during Validation conversations. These women found it difficult to facilitate the conversation while at the same time controlling their emotional reaction to what was being said. These meetings required women to isolate what was being said from how it impacted their Working Draft. I remember an experiment that did not go as planned. Without being ready for this, I could have easily caved on my hypothesis. I met with a local college president to learn about how her institution created new courses. I wanted to test an idea about creating a curriculum tied to women's development. The president did not share my enthusiasm for the topic nor was she very generous with information. It was not a great meeting. Yet while the meeting did not meet my objective, I still learned a fair amount. Most importantly, the meeting did not influence my interest in or commitment to my Working Draft. The structure of Validation helped me understand that the meeting could only generate data, not offer a conclusion about my idea. The structure put the decision squarely in my camp.

We are all better able to manage these conversation traps if we are prepared. Many women favored previously rehearsed conversation prompts to help them manage the conversations. Several are listed below. One may be useful as you prepare to meet with others to discuss your Validation activities.

Listening and Understanding:

1) *Ask Why.* Explore why someone has a particular reaction or point of view. Simply ask *why?* The question can also buy valuable time for the facilitator to right herself in a conversation. For those who might be concerned about the simplicity of this approach, let me offer the following to debunk the concern. Over the last 20 years, businesses have adopted the Japanese practice of asking the *5 Why's.* The *5 Why's* is a technique created by Toyota manufacturing that assists employees in identifying the root cause of a problem. Employees repeatedly ask why until a greater and greater understanding of the issue emerges. Since its origination, the *5 Why's* have become a cornerstone of Six Sigma, a broadly used business methodology focused on eliminating manufacturing defects.[7]

2) *Utilize Trial Restatements or Teachbacks*: Restate what you believe you heard the speaker say. This technique can assist you in fully understanding a speaker's intent. Say, "Let me repeat what I've just heard." Or, "I want to make sure that I understand what you are saying…" These prompts can require your speaker to restate their original point using a different approach. It also helps you confirm the key points that she is trying to convey.

3) *Useful Phrases:* Prepare a few phrases in advance of any interactions that can help you manage the conversation and understand the speaker's intent. For example, "Can you help me understand that more fully?" or "Can you put that in a layperson's terms?" In preparation for your meetings, be ready with several of these that sync with your speaking style. This work will help you focus more on the conversation instead of preparing your next question. It can also give you a welcome opportunity to catch your breath as your speaker restates her point.

I would recommend that you spend time thinking through your readiness to listen. Where possible, use proven techniques and be aware of common pitfalls. Make sure that you rely on your Working Draft as you filter what you hear from others. Invariably what you may hear can cause you to revisit some or all of the assumptions you made in Envision. If so, The Transitioning Process asks that you take the time to refine your initial thinking prior to proceeding with further Validation activities.

A Refinement Loop

The Refinement loop is an opportunity to cycle through the process repeatedly until the output feels right. The loop connects the work of Envision with Validate. The loop helps women integrate the learning from the Validation Phase and assess its impact on the initial hypothesis developed in Envision. When the output of the two are not in sync, the process is ready to support another cycle of inquiry and validation.

The Transitioning Process

The Transitioning Process's second phase, Validation, is a set of iterative tools designed to assist women as they refine the output from Envision. The toolkit is comprised of conducting experiments, exercising voice, developing stories, and leveraging people. The activities typically test the external manifestation of transition or those elements most visible to others. Its design positions women for success by relying on tools that break down the overall task of transition into smaller executable steps. It also reduces risk to women by addressing head-on those characteristics that make transition gendered, like voice or lack of recognition. Women self-select which tools to deploy during this phase based upon their Working Draft. Women need to keep in mind that listening and understanding provide the key to integrating real learning into their process and benefitting from the experience of others.

What stands in the way of this exciting work focused on realizing our fullest selves? Our next discussion about barriers may be helpful in answering that question. Barriers are a common part of the transition experience.

SECTION 3

Navigating Transition

CHAPTER 8

Barriers to Transition

Early in my transition, it seemed as if I could not walk a step without encountering a barrier. Most came in the form of expectations of others about what I should or could do. I felt admonished, judged, marginalized, or worse—pushed to pretend as if nothing was happening. This maelstrom deposited me on the doorstep of barriers. I wanted to understand them more and their role in my transition.

I was not alone in experiencing barriers. Cricket, a technology start-up veteran and mother of two college-aged sons, said of the barriers in her transition, "I am my own barrier, and it's because I'm standing there saying, 'What do I really want to do next?' It's a very uncomfortable place to be in." She had a long track record of success as a systems engineer and project manager. "I am used to going 80 hours a week. We're used to working. We're used to structure. I feel like I'm swimming in the Atlantic Ocean without a safety net." Even though it was scary, Cricket stayed true to her decision to answer the question. She needed to. There was no turning back. "I like what I do. Am I passionate about it? I need to rediscover that passion. I think the corporate world has sucked a lot out of many of us. We've given so much. And I think I want to find something where I can give my passion, but really feel like I'm getting something in return."

Cricket's decision to transition was very different from a change she had made 25 years earlier when she had to look for a job. "We were struggling to make payments on the mortgage." Now, she was "pausing." Her trigger was an unexpected job loss. "I haven't told my brother, and we're very close." Her brother had been with the same company for 25 years. "It's been four months. I'm just going to hear the same old thing, 'What are you going to do?'" She was fatigued by that line of questioning. She heard it constantly from herself.

Cricket learned new things about herself almost from the start in transition. "I'm taking every opportunity to help someone else. It increases my passion. It's very interesting. I should have been doing this all along." I was surprised by how she talked about her barrier. It differed quite a bit from my own experience.

This chapter looks at barriers more completely. We consider four barriers as examples in an effort to raise our awareness of the presence of barriers in our transitions. The chapter concludes with a discussion of approaches that I found useful when encountering barriers while transitioning.

Barriers: Friend or Foe?

A barrier is something that stops us from moving in a desired direction. A mortgage payment. A new boss. A husband. An ex-husband. A desired credential. A fear. They often take the form of "I can't because..." Have you ever heard yourself say something like that? I have. I wondered about these barriers and how we could be successful with transition in light of them.

Everyone's experience of barriers differs. Some women looked at barriers as an insurmountable gate—requiring or causing a full stop. Others experienced barriers as motivators—simply a hurdle to overcome. Many viewed barriers through a more combative lens—ready to take up arms against the infiltrator at a moment's notice. Regardless of which stance women favored, I was amazed at how often they described the barriers as self-imposed. I frequently heard, "All barriers are internal." I remember thinking as I listened to these women, "What about the widowed mother of three whose barrier to transition was very practical, college tuitions?" Internal or not, have we not all at this point in our life overcome at least one barrier?

Barriers are common, complex, and highly personal. They are a frequent companion to transition. They can present themselves at a transition's beginning as much as they can closer to its end. Susan, a parent of a young son and an only child whose parents had both died, identified two barriers that were complex and unique to her own experience. She chose transition after deferring it for almost a decade. Susan encountered all sorts of barriers during that time—financial responsibilities, societal and familial expectations. She said, "I think the barrier was probably my husband's job. Once he was established, I felt that I could jump out." Susan was spirited and very conscientious. She wore a brightly colored tunic as we sat in a coffee shop on the outskirts of Dallas's sprawling metropolis. She and her husband had worked hard to buy a home in Plano, TX and to establish themselves in that community.

"And as sad as it may seem, it was a barrier while my parents were alive because I think they would have said, 'Well, we sent you to medical school, why aren't you a doctor?' There came a point after they died when I could do whatever I wanted." Susan knew for a long time that she wanted out of medicine. She liked the sciences and eventually found her way to the R&D arm of a medical device company. Was there more to the barriers she listed? What about confidence? In listening to Susan, there was no question that her confidence had grown in the time since she'd established roots in Dallas. Was that a barrier too . . . one that perhaps she was even unaware of?

The nature of barriers seems to change over time. This dynamic nature may offer us an important opportunity to reframe the role of barriers in our transition. Meredith, a divorced women in her mid-fifties, shared a surprising conclusion about a barrier she had long held on to. It was one of several gates that she worked through as she transitioned. "The big shift for me was letting go of just going after the paycheck. I always went after that because I needed that security. The shift for me was just recognizing that the security was all illusion. And when I started letting go, I realized that the security I sought wasn't really gaining me the traction for joy or however you want to label it. It led me to explore other avenues that I had previously ignored."

Our experience of barriers is complex, highly individual, and varies widely. We all react differently to them. Women like Meredith and Susan and Cricket convinced me that my value add would not be from classifying barriers for women in transition. After all many psychologists, scholars, and academics have already done that. Instead their perspectives helped me see that the real value for me related to barriers was in exploring how we could be successful with transition in their presence.

Raising Our Awareness of Barriers

There are no *model* barriers that I discovered for transition or that are related to its triggers. For example, I cannot say to you, "Here is the barrier you will most likely encounter in a transition triggered by divorce" or "by childbirth" or "by searching for greater meaning in your career choices." This absence makes it more difficult to raise our awareness of the barriers that might be at play in transition. We can, however, be more mindful of the things that may stop us from moving in a desired direction. I would like to spend a moment exploring this mindful approach to our potential barriers by talking through four barriers that I heard repeatedly in my research. I chose these four because women raised them over and over again, not because they are representative of all women's experience. These four barriers are society's expectations, negative self-talk, lack of support, and time.

Society's Expectations

Societal expectations can be a barrier to transition. As we learned in our discussion about male norms and societal standards in chapter 4, these expectations are a set of beliefs about what we *"should do."* Most of us internalize these beliefs unknowingly, which in turn makes them very difficult to recognize or be aware of. I became aware of societal expectations unexpectedly and as a result learned an enormous amount about their role in my transition.

For a long time, I believed that I had somehow skirted above or around societal expectations. I did not believe that I existed within their clutches. After all, I successfully lived under the mantra "you can be anything you want to be." That phrase was present in my home growing up, as much as it was throughout my education and work life. It had given me the confidence to pursue a host of exciting and different activities as I shaped my career. It was not until my transition that I became aware of societal expectations in a different way. Was this maybe because I was stepping outside of them for the first time? All of a sudden I was in the middle of a perfect storm of expectations about parenting, working, and participating in my community.

A conversation with a colleague introduced me for the first time to just how such expectations were at play for me. One day I called a grad school classmate of mine with whom I had not talked in years. I wanted to get his perspective on an issue that I was researching on behalf of an entrepreneurial start-up with which I was working. He worked in the start-up's target industry. Since we had not talked in a long time, he started off by telling me what he was up to. Then it was my turn.

I spent a few minutes bringing him up to speed on the exciting portfolio of projects that I had underway. These included working with female-led start-ups, serving on the Board of Trustees of a $1.5 billion health-care company, and authoring a blog, for which I had just started some additional research. I was thrilled to be talking coherently about this portfolio. It had taken years to assemble and get underway. It was the most tangible example to date of my transition.

He listened. Or so I thought. As soon as I stopped talking, he said, "So you're a stay-at-home mom?" I was speechless. And angry.

Time has allowed me to think differently about that call. He unknowingly gave me a gift. He pushed me so far that day that he finally helped me understand societal expectations. Remember, I had lived by the statement "you can be anything you want." I thought I understood what it meant. But it was not until I was faced with the statement's undoing that I really understood it. My friend taught me that the place I had to start was recognizing that no one other than myself might understand the value of what I choose. It would be just me. I had to be ok with that. I realized too that my mantra of "anything I wanted to be" had operated—albeit creatively—within a narrow band of very acceptable roles that society recognized. Start-up CEO. Fortune 500 executive. MBA. Transition was taking me outside that narrow band for the first time. If *I* believed in the value of what I choose, that would have to be ok—regardless of the reactions of colleagues, friends, and family members.

Societal expectations as a barrier can take on many forms. Angela spoke of her transition by addressing this barrier head-on. She had served in a visible administrative role for a well-known academic institution for more than 14 years. She took her career seriously and had performed at an outstanding level. During her tenure, her performance was rewarded again and again with new responsibility and raises. She was well put together and looked composed in spite of the near-torrential rain on the day we met. She said of expectations and barriers, "It's kind of hard to *forge* a path on your own. For a long time I couldn't say, 'I want to be like this.' I didn't know what the answer was going to be for me. It is so much easier to follow *the* path that everyone follows. It's really hard to say, 'No, I'm not going to do that.'" For a long time she ignored her instincts that she was bored. Eventually she gave in. Even though she was successful and admired at work, she grew more and more disconnected from the work she performed. These feelings happened during a time when she and her female partner were having trouble. She reasoned that her delay in addressing her instincts was tied to her fear of being unsuccessful professionally at a time when there was so much uncertainty in her personal life. She concluded of her experience, "It's hard to say, 'This is really what I want' when there is no set path."

Gloria Steinem referenced societal expectations as a barrier she overcame in her own life in her remarks at an event sponsored by The Commonwealth Institute.[1] She said, "In my early forties, I realized I was very concerned about what this one or that one might think. Then I realized that they weren't really listening to me. At that point, I figured that I might as well say what was on my mind." And so it went. When she began to overwrite societal expectations, she gave voice to a generation.

Has what you "should do" ever played into your decision about re-examining the assumptions that lie at the heart of transition?

Negative Self-Talk

Our own internal talk track may play a role in our decisions to engage in transition. In my research, women often referenced continuous and damaging self-talk as a barrier in their transition, particularly in its earliest stages. We are all too aware of this element of ourselves. Are you able to recognize it and its potential impact on your decisions?

One woman, Roberta, shared a story about a cycle during which self-talk impeded not only her progress but her belief of what might be possible. She was in her mid-fifties and lived with her husband in San Diego. She said, "I think my barriers are all internal. I didn't reach out to people. Why? I was so embarrassed." She went through a very painful period during which she continuously cycled through a negative monologue in her head. Her transition's trigger was an unexpected job loss after more than 15 years with the same employer. She chided herself internally for not being "the intelligent woman that I always thought I had been." It took more than six months for the constant internal barrage of *failure* to lessen. Her transition also helped her recognize how she had prioritized the expectations of others. "I ignored my instincts." After a transition lasting more than a year, she said, "I think I have more confidence now that what I want for myself is enough. Instead of valuing what other people think of me. I'm saying, "OK, no. That's not what I want for myself. This is what I want."

How does your internal talk track affect your beliefs about the viability of your dreams or the potential to live the life you have imagined?

Lacking Support Structures

Support structures play an important role in our decisions related to transition and transitioining, as we saw in chapter 4. Their absence can be damaging. In my research, women talked about support structures—most often, by their absence. Like societal expectations, this factor is often difficult to see. The affirmation derived from these structures is fundamental to our ability to envision our fullest selves. The absence of these structures was cited as a barrier by many, many women.

Mary, an early forties stay-at-home mom, had no visible means of support at the outset of her transition. She said, "Sometimes it's hard to talk to the people who you are closest to about things. Even though they love you and support you. They are judgmental." She withdrew from the full-time workforce after her youngest started to struggle in school. Thanks to her children and family and their demands, she had a busy nonstop lifestyle. She relied on those closest to her for many things, but realized that they were not able to serve in a supporting role in her transition. "If you say something when you are in the phase of still trying to figure it out, and someone says, 'You are dreaming,' it is difficult to rebound," she said. "On my best days it's like, 'Wait a minute, yes, I could do it.' In order for this to even ever happen, I first have to start with a dream of it."

She knew she needed to seek out other people beyond the interactions she had had with her husband and family. "They have different mental models for how they think about things. Like your husband loves you and supports you. But you know if he has a different way of thinking than you do, even though he doesn't mean to, he'll discourage you."

How would you characterize the availability of support structures for yourself in your life? Can you imagine that their presence or absence may influence your willingness to undertake transition?

Time

I think all of us can relate to time as a barrier. After all, have you ever voiced time as a reason you could not do something important? Time seems to take on different profiles as a barrier in transition. Most women likened it to a gate, impeding their ability to start or to execute a transitioning task. Time also took on dimensions, like value, in some instances, as in "this idea isn't a good idea because it would take too much time." Time seemed to have a quality dimension as well, particularly in those most interested in transition due to retirement. For these women, time presented itself as a qualifier, "I am only looking for something for the next five to ten years." How aware are you of time's role in your decision to re-examine your assumptions or to dedicate yourself to transitioning's steps?

I met Veronica at in time when she was very sad. We took a walk through her town's conservation area. It was densely wooded. A perfect fall day. She initiated transition reluctantly after being "near crushed" under the pressure of her life. "Something had to give," she said. That something was her job, which had served as a big part of her identity. She quit her job almost a year before her widowed father passed away. She was 43. She had siblings. Even so, Veronica took the lead in managing the details. By her description, her siblings were unraveling all throughout her father's illness. Prior to her dad's death, she commuted regularly back and forth between her home in Westchester County, New York, and Connecticut, where her father lived. Her three children, husband, and job all morphed in response to her father's changing care needs.

Time was a major barrier. "With all of this, how could I possibly think about what might be next?" she asked. Although she knew things were not right on many levels, she noted, "I could barely keep my head above water." His illness lasted several years. Now, after his death she was mired in the details of his estate. Time still served as a barrier.

Can you identify how time impacts you and your decisions?

Barriers are likely present for many of us, even in ways we are not entirely aware of. In thinking about barrier's role in transition, our first step needs to be, to become aware of them. They may be persistent, like Veronica's relationship with time, or my very real fear of isolating silence that I mentioned earlier. Regardless of their profile, I found it useful to begin to raise my awareness of barriers, being mindful of their presence. I was not on the hunt to solve them. But by raising my awareness, I began to have a greater ability to think about them and their potential impact on my decisions.

Barriers and Transition's Progress

Barriers can be all around us. Recognizing them and their potential impact on our decisions is important in transition. Can we be successful with transitioning if we encounter barriers? I think the answer is emphatically yes, although there are some useful techniques that might make it a lot easier. I have found four worth noting: creating distance; focusing on small achievable wins; reframing the experience of barriers—*as if*; and repositioning barriers as learning tools.

Creating Distance—A Meditative Technique

Similar to our experience of emotions in chapter 3, our experience of barriers can benefit from creating distance between us and the barrier. If you have ever participated in a yoga class, the technique is similar to yoga's most basic step, drawing awareness to your breath. This yoga basic brings our attention to the breath as it travels into and out of our body. In a breathing exercise we raise our awareness to the breath at first, not trying to change it. So, too, in creating distance between ourselves and the barriers we encounter in transition. This technique asks us to objectively look at a feeling or issue by putting distance between ourselves and the issue. We observe it. The technique then allows us to think around, reframe, and potentially challenge the issue. Each of these steps offers us the possibility to act.

The distance technique asks a woman to become aware of or observe her barrier or issue, thereby creating distance between who she is and the issue. For example, if a woman decides that she cannot pursue a dream because she is not competent enough, the technique would give her distance between herself and this barrier thought. "When you can look at something, then by definition it is separate from who you are at your core. You are having this thought, it's not having you," said Louisa Mattson, PhD, a business psychologist and partner at Essex Partners in Boston. "Because you are no longer swallowing it hook, line, and sinker, you are no longer at its mercy. You thus have greater freedom to respond to your barrier in a new way." In our example, the woman could challenge the all-or-nothing quality of the thought that she is "not competent." Distance may help her ask questions of herself like, How has she acted competently in the past? or How might she take steps to move toward greater competency going forward? "The technique helps you see that you are 'bigger' than this thought or feeling," said Mattson. "It gives you space and frees you up to respond instead of just reacting."

Suzanne, like many women with whom I worked, worried about how her transition would express itself to others. She had been a stay-at-home mom for close to three years, after an illness caused her to step away from full-time work. She took advantage of the break to rethink several assumptions. While thankful for the time, she was anxious to get back to work.

She and I talked the night before she was scheduled for a big interview. She had had a string of unsuccessful interviews with other prospective employers. She really hoped that this one would work out. She was nervous. We spent time on the phone practicing interview questions in preparation for the next day. At one point she said, "I've been out so long, there must be something wrong with me."

Once she voiced this issue, we abandoned the interview prep and turned to the distancing technique. The distance she was able to create between herself and the concern gave her a degree of control. We used that control to discuss how she might respond in an interview should questions about her transition come up. We also used that control to talk about why she felt the way she did.

Creating distance between potential barriers and ourselves will not eliminate barriers. However, it might help women objectify barriers and gain more freedom in thinking about how to address them. This method can assist us in the process of transitioning while barriers are present for us.

Focus on Small Achievable Goals

The second useful technique for transitioning in the presence of barriers involves deconstructing the barrier and working on its smaller parts one at a time. Once we are aware of a barrier, this technique gives us an opportunity to reframe it. Often this technique helps us think of new ways to work with the barrier because it now is not viewed as a single monolithic issue. First, we break it down. Then, we look at its smaller pieces. These individually may generate ideas or help neutralize the impact that the barrier had presented. One by one we make progress.

I was introduced to an illustration of this technique one afternoon at an open practice for the Boston Celtics. [2] I went with my son and daughter. Assistant coach Kevin Eastman talked to attendees about the team's playing strategy. He said that their objective was not to win games or championships. Instead it was to win as many three- to four-minute game segments as possible. The team broke down each game into a series of three- to four-minute segments. Their objective was to win as many of these as they could. Imagine an NBA franchise coach focusing on something other than winning games or championships.

Veronica, who was mired in the details of her dad's illness and death, found this approach surprisingly useful. Her instincts led her to sequentially approach transition once she could solve for her biggest barrier, time. "Finish the family stuff and then move on," she said of her plan. Even she had to concede, "Breaking it down could allow me to start." Time was her barrier. She could easily see how she might dedicate a car ride between Connecticut and Westchester County to thinking about Envision's Fast First Draft questions. Dismantling the barrier of time gave her an element of control that she was previously unaware of.

Positioning barriers into smaller, more approachable parts may prove useful in transition, particularly for those barriers that feel large and immobile. Deconstructing a barrier into smaller parts can allow us to bring new energy to our awareness of the barrier. It will not solve for the barrier. What it might do—similar to distancing—is give us more freedom to explore how it is impacting us.

Adopt an "As If" Approach

Our transition's progress in light of barriers may benefit from adopting an "as if" brainstorming technique. With this technique we isolate the barrier and explore what our transition might look like without it. Through it, we further raise our awareness of the barrier and its potential impact on our decisions. This technique can generate new thinking about the barrier and help us understand it further. The technique is fashioned on a facilitation technique that I have used countless times with my teams in the business world to assist them in thinking through a problem. Answer the question, "What would you do if (fill in barrier) wasn't there?" Anchor your thoughts on an "as if" state, as if your barrier was no longer present.

This technique may be familiar to many. Derivatives of it are often used to isolate the role of financial barriers in decision-making, as in, "How would you answer the Fast First Draft questions if you no longer needed to pay the mortgage?" The technique causes you to reframe the barrier that your mortgage represents to your dreams.

The technique asks you to explore a "what if" state that eliminates or isolates the barrier. It will not eliminate the barrier. But it may provide you with a further awareness of it and give you more perspective about its influence on your decisions.

Repositioning for Learning

We may benefit from exploring the purposes that barriers serve in our transition. This technique acknowledges that barriers, while often perceived as obstacles, may in fact serve as oracles. This approach will ask us to go even further than the distancing exercise. The distancing exercise asks us to put distance between who we are and the issue, objectifying it. In this step, we ask about the purpose of the distanced issue. We ask, "What purpose could this barrier be serving for me?" There are all sorts of roles that the barrier could be serving: it could be protecting us from something; it could be distracting us from something. This technique is challenging, particularly because it is nearly impossible to use in real time. However, I have found the technique useful in hindsight by examining some of my decisions from the earliest stages of transition.

Earlier, I told you that I had a false start to my transition. It occurred just after my dad died, five years before my official transition would begin. I was commuting back and forth to Dallas with two children under two years old. I had come late to parenting—never stopping for a moment to consider not working now that I had children. I did not think— perhaps naively—that it would impact my passion. My passion in those days expressed itself in my being fully immersed in entrepreneurial start-ups. I loved the energy and the ambiguity. I was a bit marooned in the large corporation that had bought my company. What did I do? I changed jobs. I joined a colleague who was also an entrepreneur in an even larger corporation. That decision sent me on a five-year cycle of intense demands on my time—not all that different from the pace that I had kept in my start-up world. The one difference? The demands on my time mushroomed, thanks to my entry into motherhood and parenting.

Using the lens of learning, could my pace—intense, relentless—have been a barrier? Did it protect me from some more profound questions that I was not yet ready to answer about my identity? If I adopt this view that barriers may teach us something, I might interpret this period as one during which I made circumstantial changes to protect me from the real work on identity that I was not yet ready for.

This technique—exploring barriers for what they might teach us—is interesting and difficult. It does not lead to instantaneous answers. Their correctness is unknowable. What it can do, though, is introduce a new set of questions, which in turn can help move our transitions forward. Was the pace that I created a shield to give me time until I was comfortable enough to ask more questions about what might be next for me? These questions themselves were useful. They helped me evaluate some decisions I had made in the face of barriers. They gave me the confidence to ask even bigger questions of myself in transition.

Barriers to Transition

We encounter all sorts of barriers as we proceed through transition. Some are self-imposed, while others we view as rigidly introduced by society. Regardless of their source or profile, I found it useful to raise my awareness of them, and employ techniques so that I could continue my transition's progress in their presence. With barriers, there is no silver bullet, but taking the time to understand them can offer us more freedom to explore what transition might mean for us. Barriers can likely offer us valuable input into our transition decisions. At the very least, they may help us with one of the most important steps in transition, the decision to begin.

CHAPTER 9

Getting Started

"We always come back to ourselves, only better," said Kailee, a transition veteran. She and I were talking on the phone. I had called her because I had hit a wall. She offered the remark as I wondered out loud, "What am I doing?" Her optimism and calm manner talked me off the ceiling that day. Kailee was no shrinking flower. She had transitioned twice, once when a miscarriage and other health problems forced her to rethink work, and a second time when she adopted a child as a single mom. I valued her advice and loved how much she believed in the process that I was going through.

The reason for my call was simple. I had been turned down for a part-time job that I had recently interviewed for. It was a great role. A perfect experiment. I knew on some level that there would be other roles. It did not have to be this one. What I could not wrap my head around was, "Did it mean that I would have to start over?" That was the real elephant in the room. I had an awful feeling in the pit of my stomach when talking with Kailee. I wanted to avoid starting again at any cost. I wondered out loud if the rejection translated into a grade for my Working Draft. Did it mean that I would have to start again?

As I thought about it, I realized that, no, the rejection had nothing to do with the validity of my overall direction. Yes, it did offer me some valuable lessons that I would apply to the next interview. But this was not a grading of my entire endeavor. It was a data point. A single instance. What the loss did do, was put another important topic on my radar screen, "starting." Six months after that call, I would begin my research with my women interviewees. Thanks to the call, I would be listening differently about "starting."

This chapter is all about getting started. Getting started can happen at the beginning when we decide to initiate a transition. It can also feel as if it is happening again and again as we go through the cycles of experimentation. If my experience is at all representative, starting deserves attention. This chapter looks at the individual nature of our paths through transition, some lessons learned about starting, and a few things to help us get started.

A Context for Starting

Do you remember the Transition Anatomy with its three parts: a trigger, a decision, and an action? Would it surprise you that it plays a fundamental role in starting? The anatomy can help dispel fears about what lies ahead and reduce the uncertainty that surrounds starting (see Figure 9.1). What is it about this anatomy that can be so helpful?

Knowledge of the anatomy—which serves as a framework for transition—can help us understand what is ahead. With it, we see the entire cycle, not just the moment we are in. This context helps as we interpret events in our lives, like triggers. For example, a woman can ask herself a broader set of questions with knowledge of the anatomy when she experiences triggers like an unexpected job loss or an intentional trigger like a remarriage. Ideally, this knowledge can help women keep away from their instinctive first reactions, like the too familiar feelings of inadequacy or self-doubt experienced by many. For me, this knowledge helped me quickly reboot my efforts in the wake of rejection. Without it, I would have been less able to view the experience as a data point meant to validate or invalidate my Working Draft.

The anatomy can also be useful in understanding how each individual's experience of transition differs. Everyone moves through the three parts of

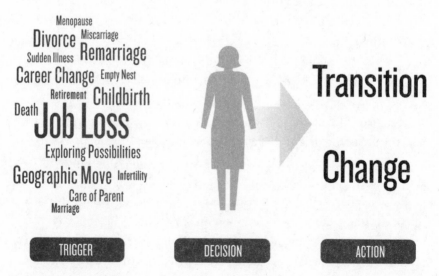

Figure 9.1 Transition's anatomy.

the anatomy in her own way. This variability can appear stark, especially if we focus on triggers and decisions. For some, the progression from trigger to decision can feel slow and evolutionary. It can occur over a period of months or years. There can be multiple triggers. I heard comments like "there were signs. I ignored them" by women in this category. At the other extreme are women who move quickly to a decision following a trigger. Comments like "my husband died, I had no other choice" were made by women in this category. Often for these women the decision to proceed is laser sharp and met with what feels like instantaneous clarity, despite the pervasive uncertainty over what might be ahead after the decision step. Differences are also present in one's experience of the last stage of the anatomy, the act of transitioning. We choose our own pace and scope for transitioning. Some choose to move quickly. Others over a decade or more. Regardless of the individual decisions, all transitions go through the basic three-part anatomy.

Our knowledge about the anatomy can also reduce concerns that we may have about the circular pattern of our transition. Women may Ping-Pong back and forth between triggers and the potential for a decision for many years... never really reaching a decision. This pattern may repeat itself until a woman becomes aware of her ability to make a decision. Some will encounter this very pattern and decide not to transition. The difference is important. At transition's core—regardless of the route—lies a decision. A choice.

The anatomy highlights the most significant element of transition, a conscious act. A decision. Transition will not happen passively. Many women have questioned me on this point. They wonder, "What about those women for whom transition is evolutionary?" At some point—even in a small way—a woman needs to be willing to explore her assumptions. It is that willingness that serves as a decision. Sometimes women are only comfortable exploring tiny elements of their assumptions, a piece of their identity or a single value that no longer seems aligned. It does not really matter how much of an assumption is at play—the whole thing or just a small part. There is, however, an active choice, to re-examine.

Transition's anatomy is a useful resource in support of the first, toughest step, starting. Our next section explores the lessons learned related to starting that are shared by those women who have made this choice.

Lessons Learned

If starting can be such an impediment, what can we learn from others who have already done so? Women in my research shared many lessons. Four lessons learned were related to starting and may be useful as you plan your first steps.

Manage Our Bias Toward Action

Woman are incredible mobilizers. We can coordinate weekend tournaments for the girls' softball team, manage our extended family's annual reunion, and coordinate meal delivery for the family down the street whose mom is being treated for cancer, all the while holding a full-time job and keeping some semblance of an evening meal on the table nightly. These terrific skills, which I refer to as our bias toward action, tend to work against us in the earliest stages of transition. Why? Transition asks us to stop in order to start, a completely disarming concept for many.

Managing this bias toward action can help us more fully execute the earliest stages of transition. The steps of Envision require self-discovery and thought. Keeping this lesson in mind may help women be more successful with these self-reflective steps. The lesson may also reduce the risk of women skipping altogether the earliest steps—believing in fact that they already know the answers. Estelle, a retired sales operations professional from the high-tech industry, said of transition's earliest steps, "It was a creative void that opened up a lot of things for me." She credited this creative void with exponentially increasing the value of her transition. In fact, Anne LeClaire, author of *Listening Below the Noise: A Meditation on the Practice of Silence*,[1] established a great image for our work in Envision: "It is stopping and paying attention that awakens us."[2] While few of us will be able to stop entirely, transition will require us to stop what we are used to doing at least partially and dedicate time, energy, and emotional attention to transitioning.

Adopt a Key Phrase

The second *starting* lesson learned is to create and adopt an introductory phrase that can be used repeatedly during transition. Women were quick to get this on the list, thanks to countless uncomfortable stories related to social interactions during transitioning. For example, have you ever been asked, "What do you do?" following a personal or professional change? Were you able to answer it as elegantly as you would have liked? This lesson learned asks that you create a key phrase to use in response to this question while you are in transition. The phrase can neutralize social tensions and work as a useful engagement platform for your transition.

Kate, a single early-forties woman, recounted, "I always tell people the easiest time I had communicating what I did was when I was the most miserable." She holds a master's in fine arts. "When I was a business manager at a large arts organization here in the city, I always got a very positive response from people when I introduced myself in professional situations or even at cocktail parties. People put me in a certain box." We had coffee at a noisy independent coffee bar in New York City. "I think it's the same way a lot of people think about choosing a business school. A lot of people say that it's worth going to a name brand because that's what gives you credibility in the marketplace."

She went on to share a painful and embarrassing moment. "I went to an invitation-only networking event. The attendees, all female, were positioned as the 50 up-and-coming leaders in the city. And there I am with doctors and lawyers and people who are on a path, and I don't know how to define myself." She had resigned from her job six months prior. "I think that you almost—whether it's your insecurity or whether it's actually real—feel judged by people. I think women in particular look for these anchors professionally that give us credibility, that we often feel we don't have on our own, for better or for worse."

Kate was not alone in her thinking about others' response to her decision. Her trigger had been a belief that something more was possible for her. It was a difficult decision and one that she wavered on for a long time. She added, "I remember being vulnerable when it came to my turn that night. I thought everyone in the room must have thought, 'Have you been fired?' They must have thought something had gone off the tracks, right?" Kate was embarrassed and self-critical of her behavior that evening. When it was her turn, she offered a jumble of past experiences as her introduction.

To help in Kate-like moments, we need to create a simple phrase. If your transition has advanced to the Envisioning stage, you can rely on an excerpt from your Working Draft (see chapter 6). If it has not, you can rely on the following suggestions to help you create an initial phrase.

When crafting your phrase, use verbs like investigating, considering, or unearthing, which suggest impermanence and action. This communicates to listeners that you are *in process*. The phrase should also contain a statement of interest. "I'm exploring non-full-time work options." "I'm exploring postretirement gigs." "I'm exploring re-entry strategies given that I've been out of the workforce for many years." "I'm investigating what it is like to be a single parent." One woman who wanted to re-engage in the workforce while her transition was still ongoing said, "I am interviewing my next employer." Some women derived comfort from anchoring the phrase with prior roles. For example, "I am exploring post-retirement gigs in environmental policy after a career in the law." Or, "I am exploring non-full-time work options after finalizing my recent divorce." The statements are designed to engage others in conversation. Their objective is not—at least in the formative stages of transition—to communicate your transition's desired outcome. Think of it as another means for experimentation, one that can supply immediate feedback and useful information.

You can craft an initial introductory phrase by answering the questions in the box below. It should communicate that you are investigating new opportunities and welcome feedback and input from others.

Developing Your Introductory Phrase :

- What areas or topics would you like to explore in your transition?
- What areas would you most like to impact?
- What problem—or types of problems—are you trying to solve?
- What topic or area would be most useful to learn more about?
- If you could name one thing that you love doing, what would it be?
- What value would you most like to deliver to others?

Once drafted, practice the phrase prior to needing to use it. Update it as you proceed through transition.

As I have already told you, I used "I am on sabbatical," as my short phrase early in my transition, to disastrous results. When I changed it to "I am exploring my interest in women's development," everything changed. I could have used anything after the word exploring—exploring the man in the moon—it did not really matter. What did matter was that the statement served as a means of engagement for those with whom I was speaking. It also purposely avoided a fixed outcome or destination for my transition. In response, listeners began offering perspectives that were both unexpected and helpful.

Change Your Mind-Set

The third *starting* lesson learned asks that you to change your mind-set away from destination and toward experimentation and learning. We are conditioned in our society to focus our efforts on singular outcomes, like destinations. With this lens comes binary vocabulary—success or failure. Did you get there? Or not? We effortlessly create these "on" or "off" mental models every day. This focus, while a useful motivator, can put an undue burden on the outcomes and risk extinguishing learning altogether. By contrast, this lesson asks us to adopt an experimentation mind-set that helps focus on questions, not their answers.

Most of us on the planet know the story of Steve Jobs, the enigmatic figure behind Apple. Early in his life, he adopted a mantle of experimentation that he later credited with much of his success—success that included the Macintosh, Pixar blockbusters like *Toy Story*, the Apple Stores, iTunes, the iPod, and the iPad.[3] "Much of what I stumbled into by following my curiosity and intuition turned out to be priceless later on," he said during a commencement speech at Stanford University in 2005.[4] He was referencing a period during which he dropped out of college and then hung around the Reed College campus to explore courses that appeared interesting to him but would not have been part of his core curriculum. He credited experimentation with enormous value. "Of course it was impossible then to connect the dots. (The benefit) was very, very clear looking backwards ten years later."[5]

Would it surprise you that I heard the same reliance on experimentation and learning as expressed by Jobs many times in my research? "Looking back, there is so much clarity," said Julieanne, "but going off and being an entrepreneur was never part of my program." She was an incredibly successful entrepreneur who spoke with me at her company's headquarters, a renovated mill building in southern New Hampshire. She was a physics undergraduate who graduated from Northwestern University with an MBA. She joined an auto parts manufacturer after graduating and worked there for more than ten years. She was ultimately miserable at the job, but stayed long enough to continue a series of costly and unsuccessful fertility treatments. Once she got herself away from the environment, she started a set of experiments that lasted close to two years. She did quirky things like helping a cousin renovate an old farmhouse in New England. And she did more traditional things like look for jobs. One day an acquaintance told her about a business for sale. She investigated it, but ultimately concluded that there was no need to buy a business. She could start one on her own. Julieanne credits experimentation with helping her new self evolve after a devastating personal and professional period. The best part? She found a way to embrace something that she loved, children's health, as this newer version of herself emerged.

It might sound simple, but this reframing of our approach away from success or failure and more toward experimentation and learning is significant. I have found that adopting this mind-set requires a conscious effort. Questions not outcomes. One elegant woman who participated in a Focus Group one evening summarized this mind-set by referencing the renowned German poet Rainer Maria Rilke, who said, "Live the questions now. Perhaps then, someday far in the future, you will gradually, without even noticing it, live your way into the answer."[6]

A mind-set that embraces experimentation and learning helps us begin without answers to all of the questions related to transition. It asks us to suspend the preferred societal construct of destination. If the women with whom I spoke are representative, enormous gifts await those who can make this switch.

Know Your Economics

The final *starting* lesson learned stresses the importance of pacing your transition in light of the financial responsibilities you carry. Rent payments or mortgages. Car payments. Braces for the kids. College tuitions. Health-care bills. Upcoming events, like a wedding or a down payment on a house. Retirement. What constitutes our obligations differs. The lesson challenges us to factor these responsibilities into our thinking about transition and the pace that you alone will determine.

The risk of not factoring financial obligations into your planning decisions can have a long-term impact on your financial well-being. Most women with whom I worked were very aware of this potential. Just as many, however, did not factor it into their planning. Researchers and scholars have long confirmed that a wage gap exists for women in our society. It is driven by many factors including, but not limited to, pay inequality and wage discrimination due to employment interruptions. Anne Crittenden, author of *The Price of Motherhood: Why the Most Important Job in the World Is Still the Least Valued*,[7] said it best, "I took what I thought was a relatively short break, assuming it would be easy to get back into journalism after a few years. I was wrong. As it turned out I sacrificed more than half of my lifetime earnings."[8] Massachusetts Lt. Governor Evelyn Murphy quantified this disadvantage in her exposé *Getting Even: Why Women Don't Get Paid Like Men and What to Do about It*.[9] She revealed that women face pervasive wage discrimination, which can cost women between $700,000 and $2,000,000 worth of lifetime earnings, depending on many factors, like their educational background.[10] Taking the time to understand how your long-term earnings may be impacted by your decisions is an important planning step to take prior in determining your transition's pace.

Factoring financial obligations into our pace decisions may also translate into the need for contingencies to support transition. These can take the form of savings or related support structures, like care providers for children or elders.

One contingency that too often escapes notice is how to handle credentials in light of the uncertainty that surrounds transition. Many roles in our society, from physicians to firefighters to teachers, require certifications. Triggers can lead women to exit jobs abruptly and as a result irresponsibly handle certifications. The mini lesson learned? Investigate what is minimally required to maintain your certification prior to deciding to proceed with transition. Consider undertaking whatever the minimal requirements are in order to maintain that status until you advance through the first few steps of transitioning. Even though you may swear never to return to a specific line of work, it is smart to proceed in this fashion. You may decide later to come back to the field or a related one, which could require the very same certification.

"That's how the old boys' club does it!" screamed Eunice at me as she related a conversation between herself and a former colleague. "They park certifications." She was a high-powered finance jock from an investment bank. She had been out of a work environment for several years, thanks to kids and to some other extended family issues. Eunice told me funny stories about how she got no satisfaction from decorating her house nor cooking meals. She loved to work. She was actively looking for a job. Early in her career, she had sat for the Series 7,[11] a license required to trade securities.

Her former colleague had agreed to sponsor her for a job at a boutique investment bank where he now worked. Just prior to calling me, she learned from him that she would be ineligible for the position unless she had a current Series 7 certification. Her fury was rooted in her colleague's surprise at how she had handled her certification during her absence. She learned from him that it was common practice for those—frequently men—who leave the large investment banks to sign on as *consultants* with smaller firms, if only to maintain licenses. She was livid that she did not know of this practice years before.

I am not advocating that you falsely represent your employment status to maintain licensure. What I am arguing is that you not only understand but also seriously consider maintaining minimum requirements for licensure at the outset of your transition. Many women unknowingly let certifications lapse, believing at the start of their transition that they will never return to their field.

Each of us will make different decisions about how to pace our transitions in light of financial obligations. We prioritize different things as we approach financial responsibilities. It was not lost on me as I considered transition that finances played an enabling, not a derailing, role. I was lucky that I had a financial cushion that I had built up over time. With it I could withstand a period of inconsistent earnings. This was not always true in my life, and it was not true for many of the women who participated in my research. Financial responsibilities will always be present for the great majority of us. Figuring out how to proceed with transition in light of them requires information and an open mind related to pacing.

Starting transition can be a difficult and scary step. You may find it helpful to keep in mind four starting lessons learned: managing our bias toward action, adopting a key phrase, changing your mind-set to experimentation rather than destination, and knowing your economics. Together these should help you proceed with greater confidence.

Packing Our Bags

The most light-hearted discussion that I had during my research occurred when I asked women to work with me through a hypothetical scenario. In it I asked them to pack a bag for a woman just starting out in transition. "What should we put in the bag?" I wondered. I was amazed at the tremendous breadth of responses that I got. There were tissues and chocolates and plane tickets and fitness apps. There were tangible and intangible items. There were a few that were inspirational and important: a mirror, our voice, a little structure, the ability to be present, and kindness as expressed through an open heart.

A Mirror

I was surprised that a mirror made it on the list and even more surprised as to how it was positioned. It was a "must-have" for two different reasons. A mirror was chosen for its ability to help see inside of ourselves and for its ability to help us see what others see.

One woman, Deborah, shared, "I am having a hard time with this transition. My career and accomplishments are a large part of how I see myself and the success I've had in life." She had been laid off by a long-time employer. She characterized the initial stages of her transition as "horrible, awful, ego-busting." "So it's been really, really difficult," she shared. She was a divorced woman in her late forties. Her two adult daughters lived on the East Coast, far from her Oregon home. To the bag she added "a mirror so you can really look at yourself. Or do a selfie. So you can really look at yourself and see yourself as other people see you." She was crushed by the distorted image that she believed others saw in looking at her. Her contribution of a mirror to the bag was driven by a mix of angst and deep sadness.

On the exact opposite side of the spectrum, Agnes, a woman in her early sixties, said, "A mirror. So that she could see herself reflected back to herself. And each time she looks in the mirror, she would see a more profound and exquisite part of herself." This sentiment was offered in kindness and hope. Agnes talked about a painful self-judging pattern that she held through much of her adult life. Her internal voice was a negative hypercritical companion. Her mirror was a purposeful, hard-earned gift. In putting it in the bag, Angela said, "I hope that other women can use it to see the beautiful gifts that were a part of themselves all along." For Agnes it had taken far too long to reach this conclusion.

Voice

Many research participants put a woman's "voice" in the travel bag. I was happy to hear this suggestion, particularly since this data was gathered long before I developed transition's toolkit. These women were very aware of their propensity to become quieter in vulnerable times. They desired to help other women avoid the pitfalls associated with swallowing up into themselves. This item was a simple reminder to women to be aware of and to work against a tendency to go silent in and around the circumstances of their own transitions.

Felice offered an interesting comparison about voice. Her transition was triggered by an unexpected illness for which she was diagnosed immediately after losing her husband to cancer. "Having your voice is huge. And being heard. When my husband died, everyone was sympathetic. Everybody knew he died. There was voice to that experience—even though I had to say very little. There it was. He died. Things were very different when I got sick. The diagnosis was not visible. I was silent. It was so much harder in many ways." Felice hoped that women would bring voice to their experiences—all of them, not just the good ones.

Another woman, Bethany, shared, "I've been divorced twice, and the transitions I went through with those were very difficult. The first time I was crushed because the values and my image of my life were just blown apart. The second time I had twins, and it was completely different because I had the children to think of. While in some ways I got stronger through these experiences, my voice was gone. I thought I'd failed. I was a failure. I was alone."

A Little Structure

"Be needed." It was a simple item. For these women, "a little structure" expressed itself as an opportunity to give of themselves in a predictable fashion, like volunteering. Yet there was more to it. Being needed offered these women many things: a place or time to be somewhere, deliverables, or milestones against which to measure their progress. In the face of uncertainty a little structure added enormous value. Almost without exception these women spoke of the benefit they derived from giving of themselves.

One woman, Cecilia, an early seventies mother of two grown sons, said, "This concept of being needed is the best gift." She graduated from culinary school in her early twenties before leaving the workforce after her first child was born. "I'm mentoring because I want to be needed. Finding ways to be needed while working through the transition has really helped me." She mentored youth in her community who were interested in pursuing fields in the culinary arts.

Beyond the benefit of being needed, these activities can also contribute to our transitions as validation activities, like experiments. Early in my transition I volunteered to chair a science, technology, engineering and math carnival in my town. We had things like Google Glass demonstrations and touchscreen-controlled robotics for kids and their families to play with. It was fun and enjoyable for all those who attended, including my two elementary school-aged children who helped me at the event. This simple activity surprisingly helped me identify important characteristics about work that I would factor into my Working Draft. These were energy, creativity, and ambiguity, all characteristics that I thrived on in any environment. Who knew such a noncritical event could help me isolate what would become non-negotiables as I defined what held meaning and value for me? ?

Being Present

The fourth item cited was another intangible, *being present*. To be present seemed to connote a state of mind that allowed a woman to be fully in the moment. The item was suggested as a reinforcement against the constant worries related to transitioning. For many, it was aspirational. No matter what they were doing, these women found it difficult to silence the uncertainty of transition that played over and over in their heads.

Cynthia, a late forties lifelong employee of a government contractor, said, "A friend really brought this to my attention. She was wrong by the way—but she helped me see it." Cynthia had been laid off from a very demanding job. She was the primary breadwinner in her household.

The word she used to describe her transition was "relieved." She was so relieved. She was thankful to be out of the 24–7 swirl that had been her life prior to being laid off. She retold a story of a friend who said to her, "'Oh, but you were always there. You were here at all of her major things'" referring to Cynthia's teenage daughter. This comment sent Cynthia reeling. Her friend was talking about her daughter's basketball games. She joked that in fact she was there, but constantly checking her BlackBerry when her daughter was not looking. "There is, there is being present. It's just an interesting mind shift. I am amazed at the impact it is having on me." Cynthia was thankful for this lesson as it helped her manage the uncertainty related to her work of transitioning.

An Open Heart

The final item for the bag was a wish that all women could find it in their hearts to be kind to themselves through transition. To forgive ourselves. To shrug off unexpected failures and get back up without self criticism. This sentiment was voiced by many, all of whom agreed that we are too often our own worst enemy. Women were quick to note that kindness could have a benefit in their transition if it were directed at others and at themselves. Kind eyes and an open heart remind us to suspend self-judgment and embrace the learning and gifts that can come with transition.

Starting

Once we make a decision to initiate transition, we are left with only one thing, to begin. Sounds easy, doesn't it?

We have learned an enormous amount. We understand transition and how it differs from change. We have walked through its anatomy and explored the specifics of its implementation. Even with so much information, though, the sheer act of transitioning can be unsettling and confusing. By understanding transition's anatomy, we gain insights into the individual path each of our transitions might take. So, too, lessons learned from starting can further illuminate what beginning may look like for you. We will never eliminate all the questions and apprehension related to starting. At the end of the day, we need to believe that whatever uncertainty is present will pale in comparison to the value derived from stepping forward, starting. I have found that value to be engaging and deeply enriching. Are you ready to begin?

CHAPTER 10

Your Journey

I have learned that transition offers enormous value to those who choose to engage with it. I am amazed by how consistently women voice its benefits. Of it women say things like energizing, and surprising, and empowering, and freeing. Story upon story reflected these exact sentiments. Its value is undeniable. What stands between women and realizing this value? An awareness of transition and courage to make the choice to explore it.

Tricia, a captivating early fifties woman from the Midwest, actively chose. "I got a sense of breathing for the first time," said Tricia of her transition. "I had no idea how much I was going to grow. I feel so fulfilled." I got goosebumps listening to her. Her message was potent.

Tricia arrived at transition thanks to an unintentional trigger, a job loss. After 29 years at a major packaged goods company in the Midwest, she was included in her employer's downsizing. "I'd seen the handwriting on the wall," she offered. "We had a new CEO. There were lots of changes going on," she said. "As the downsizing grew closer, invitations to critical meetings never arrived. My meetings with new leadership didn't go as well as I'd planned." She was not surprised that day when she was asked to walk down the hallway to a conference room.

Tricia was no stranger to transition. It took her 14 months to re-engage in full-time work after being laid off. Of her behavior in those intervening months, she added, "We choose how to react in every situation." As I listened to her story I could only conclude that her new job was thanks to a combination of focus, tenacity, humility, and grace. This transition was important for her. The company and her success there had been a major source of her identity for a long time. It also had served as a ballast during a difficult period. Tricia is the mother of four children, one of whom tragically passed away after a childhood illness. As she shared that element of her identity with me, her sadness spoke before she did.

"I found it best to get out of the negativity spiral and move to a state of action," she added. The negativity—described as anger, disappointment, and shame—were real. Tricia found that it was ok to feel those emotions, but dangerous to let them define her.

The undercurrent in Tricia's transitioning was choice. "We choose how we show up every day." At the outset of her transition, her choices were simple—they aligned with her personal commitment to learning and giving. "Giving to others is my dopamine," she said, referring to the neurotransmitter that influences cognition, attention, and pleasure. It was impossible not to be captivated by Tricia's energy. She was thoughtful and unwilling to compromise.

Our journey with transition starts with the choices we make—choices similar to Tricia's. What will you choose to do when faced with a trigger? Will you choose to explore the assumptions that are near and dear to you? In this chapter, we step back and review what we have learned about transition and think about why it matters.

Through the Lens of Transition

My investigation into transition started because I was wholly unprepared for the trigger that occurred on the banks of the Thames River in London when a phone call alerted me to the fact that my kindergarten daughter had been left standing alone at school dismissal time. Even though I could not define transition at that moment, I was intrigued that amid all sorts of emotions—like exhaustion and guilt and fear—I held on to a very positive belief, possibility. A belief that there was something more for me. A possibility. *Of what?* I did not know.

Nearly 12 months later, I became acutely aware of the gap in the narrative between women's progress and what was transpiring for myself and women all around me. I had always been interested in women's progress and believed that I lived its ideals. The contradictory nature of what was happening to me played out again and again as I spoke with other women. Women, capable, thinking, energetic, spirited women, introduced themselves always with qualifiers: former, part-time, stay-at-home, searching, looking, desperate, and unglued. What was happening? And why was no one talking about it?

My journey of discovery that was related to transition was born out of my interest in those very questions. Transition is not widely understood, much less talked about. We toss the word around occasionally but rarely come close to its true meaning. Transition is a process through which we re-evaluate how we make meaning in our world. It requires us to re-examine our assumptions about identity, capacity, and values. It is a choice we make when faced with the need to change. It can occur at any time over the course of a person's life. It follows a predictable set of phases, whether we are 34 or 54 or 74. In fact, transition is a normal part of adult growth and development.

Transition has a three-part anatomy. It is comprised of a trigger, a decision, and an action. All transitions share this anatomy. Triggers are the events or people or feelings that initiate a transition. Marriage. Career Changes. Menopause. Retirement. Bereavement. Childbirth. Empty Nests. Changes in health status. The types of triggers vary widely and are often visible. They are rarely one dimensional. Instead, they are made of events like job losses, but so too boredom or disillusionment over an employer's values. Decisions are less visible and require a person to act. A person cannot proceed beyond this point in the framework without actively choosing to re-examine certain assumptions. The final stage of the anatomy, the act of transitioning, is a multistep iterative process. Moving through the two earliest phases can feel evolutionary over the course of months or years. Or it can feel sudden, thanks to a certain clarity of decision triggered by unexpected events. The experience of the anatomy is highly individual.

Triggers, the lead element of transition's anatomy, are typically accompanied by emotions, thoughts and feelings—a variety of reactions herein referred to as emotions. Even though triggers vary, a common set of emotions—both positive and negative—are typically present. Emotions recur and recur and recur throughout our transitions. They can be damaging if left unchecked. We can leverage techniques, like externalization, to reduce the risk that we misinterpret emotions.. These techniques also build a competency for risk and generate a resiliency for the repetitive patterns of transition that we may experience over the arc of our lives.

Both women and men can transition. Transition is gendered because of how women respond to it. This response is influenced by how we are socialized. Our socialization has an enormous impact on who we are—and how we make meaning in our world. These influences shape how we respond to questions like "what should I do?" or "what do I want to do?" Our socialization's influence served as an important design consideration in crafting the transitioning process featured in this book

A woman can choose transition as one of many different paths open to her when she faces the need to change in her life. If a woman decides to transition, she initiates a process of transitioning. I have created an iterative two-step process to assist women with the re-examination at the heart of transition. It is designed to help women articulate their dreams and proceed through a set of actions in order to realize them. The process was informed by business models, including the Agile Software Development Methodology, in which adaptive learning cycles are prominent. I recommend that, prior to beginning the process, women assess their readiness for transition. This assessment helps a woman explore whether or not her assumptions are fixed in some way, or immutable.

The transitioning process is made up of two steps: to Envision and to Validate. The first step supports women as they gain further clarity on what holds meaning for *them*, a process whose output we refer to as the Working Draft. It is forward looking, encompassing our most authentic view of our fullest selves. The structure of the Working Draft makes important linkages between value and meaning in how women define themselves. The second step, Validate, offers a toolkit that can be deployed in testing and further refining a woman's best thinking about her future. Together, the two steps form a repetitive cycle of inquiry until a woman reaches her desired direction.

Those who transition may encounter barriers. Barriers are internal or external forces that can impede our progress. Barriers are highly prevalent. I have learned that we can go through them, over them, or around them. We can ignore them or even sit with them. Regardless of how they present themselves, they are likely something that we can learn from and use to reframe our thinking about ourselves and our transitions and the questions we need to ask ourselves in the process.

Even with this tremendous amount of understanding, transition's trickiest step can simply be starting. At its core, transition requires us to make a choice, an informed choice, to step forward into uncertainty. Even though the destination of that journey is unclear, it holds enormous potential value for those who choose it.

Are there choices you will make thanks to this broader awareness of transition?

Our Journey Together

Our understanding of transition will not give us the answer to what lies ahead for us. It can, however, do many powerful things. It can raise our awareness of the choices available to us and the road we will travel should we make those choices. It may help us reframe circumstances or events that previously stood in our way of making personal progress. It may give us comfort in knowing that there are others who have traveled this road. It may help us know what to expect around the next corner. It will undoubtedly empower us with knowledge and allow us to make an informed decision when faced with the need to change. It will undeniably lead us to understand that there is a choice to make. Our choice. A choice about what you are willing to explore. A choice that touches the very fabric of who you are.

What our understanding of transition may also do is align our voices so that we can collectively drive renewed attention to that which stands in our way. The list of those roadblocks is, sadly, very long. On it are things like unequal pay or the lack of flexible time policies; outdated institutional structures like the length of school days that end in the middle of the working day; workplace norms that discriminate overtly or covertly; or norms that leave women in the default care role for elders or other dependent family members. My hope is that with the lens of transition we become even more impatient to address these very real stumbling blocks that face women—and a growing number of men who serve in care roles. With the knowledge of transition, we can continue with our own personal development, while in parallel we work to address these pervasive and limiting societal road blocks.

My Journey

When I began this journey, I thought that transition was a process that I would go through, the operative word being *through*. It would have a beginning and an end. That felt comfortable to me. It was like many other life processes that had a cycle: college or grad school or childbirth. What I now realize is that transition never ends. Once I opened myself up to examining my assumptions and embracing learning, I realized something more valuable. The cycle is on-going. It may plateau or become inactive for a while, but it will never conclude. It will walk with me as I continue to wonder and dream and reach.

I am incredibly grateful to transition. It has deposited me in places I had never thought possible. I have lived its euphoria and its humility. It inspired me to remove boundaries and helped me give voice to that which has tremendous value and meaning to *me*. I continue transitioning. I approach it today with more courage and determination, thanks to the invaluable context about transition I now hold. My sincerest hope is that it delivers to you that which it provided me: a willingness to look for something "*more*," untethered, unencumbered, and unafraid.

Acknowledgments

This book represents the contributions and input of an enormous number of people for whom I am ever grateful. At the top of the list are the women and men who shared their expertise and transition stories with me through Focus Groups, one-on-one interviews, and online surveys. Their collective voice gave me the confidence to ask more questions of myself and of others. Even though I would like to name each individual here, I guaranteed all the participants anonymity in exchange for their participation. What I can say that is to a one, I was touched by their courage and grace. I only hope that I respond with the same openness and authenticity if I am ever asked to participate in an evolving endeavor like my research.

The next group that deserves incredible praise are my "*readers*," six women who agreed to offer feedback on an ongoing basis throughout my writing process. Together they represent a broad cross section of women's dynamic life experiences. They are: Helen Dajer, Lisa D'Allesandro DeMont, Dr. Julia Gallagher, Carol Goldberg, Barbara Kivowitz, and Marla McDonald. Each one contributed tirelessly to this effort and provided me with insightful and provocative feedback. I am thankful for their time, energy, humor, and patience as I worked through draft upon draft of each chapter. The book would not be what it is without their input. I am touched by their willingness to work with me in this fashion amid all of the demands of their busy lives. I am even more honored to know that they are each my friend.

An enormous thanks also goes to Ralph Roberto, President Keystone Partners, LLC, for his support of me and his willingness to offer his organization as a learning "lab" for this project. He, along with Betsy McCarthy,

Essex Partners, LLC; Laurie Roberts, Essex Partners, LLC; Stephanie Daniel, Keystone Partners, LLC; and Joy Giffen, Keystone Partners, LLC, contributed to my research and offered broad-based support. Ralph and his team cohosted research and connected me with subject-level experts critical to the book's argument. His organization taught me to rethink the boundaries of partnership—an area already very familiar to me at the project's outset.

A special thanks goes to Louisa Mattson, PhD, clinical psychology, and partner at Essex Partners, LLC, for her willingness to share her expertise. Louisa helped me access psychology's broad knowledge base. She also provided expert review and input on several critical issues fundamental to the book. As a non-psychology major, I relied upon Louisa's command of her subject and was grateful for her introduction to resources and individual experts.

I am forever indebted to Laurie Harting, Palgrave Macmillan, who took a risk on a first-time author with a big message. She championed the project every step of the way and educated me on the ins and outs of the unique world of publishing. I also want to acknowledge the entire team at Palgrave Macmillan, including Marcus Ballenger and Kristy Lilas, for their support of the book throughout its preproduction, production, and postproduction stages.

Special thanks go to Ursula Liff for her contributions as a research assistant and collaborator during the book's formative stages. I also need to acknowledge Lora Kratchounova, Scratch Marketing and Media, for her willingness to share her expertise early on in the book's gestation.

Thank you also to Sherry Penny, former Chancellor UMass Boston and founder of UMass Boston's Emerging Leaders Program, for her willingness to collaborate and connect me with a broad cross section of thinkers and leaders.

To the readers of Novofemina.com who listened as I talked out loud about transition. Thank you! You helped me give voice to an emergent topic that stands to benefit women broadly. Thank you for comments, encouragement, and quiet strength.

I would also like to acknowledge and thank the staff of the public libraries in Eastern Massachusetts who support the CLAMS (Cape Libraries Automated Materials Sharing) and Minute Man Library Networks.

Thank you and congratulations on the wonderful work you do in each of your respective communities.

Most especially I would like to thank my two children and my husband for their inspiration and support. I would not have been able to complete the project without their silliness, energy, and care. My daughter and son both played back to me throughout the book's creation a theme from our household: "through hard work, anyone can achieve anything they dream." What a treat to live my dream with the three of you!

To giving voice to dreams...

Notes

1 Change or Transition?

1. William Bridges, *Transitions: Making Sense of Life's Changes*, 2nd ed. (Cambridge, MA: Da Capo Press, 2004).
2. Bridges, *Transitions*, 128.
3. Bridges, *Transitions*, 129.
4. Bridges, *Transitions*, 105.
5. Bridges, *Transitions*, 17.
6. Robert Kegan, *The Evolving Self* (Cambridge, MA: Harvard University Press, 1982).
7. Kegan, *The Evolving Self*, 215 ff.
8. Sylvia Ann Hewlett, *Off-Ramps and On-Ramps: Keeping Talented Women on the Road to Success* (Boston, MA: Harvard Business School Press, 2007).
9. Hewlett, *Off-Ramps and On-Ramps*, 60–61.
10. Novofemina's Research Jam Online Survey; n = 139. For the purposes of the survey, we used a simple definition of transition: reimagine our notion of self.
11. Hewlett, *Off-Ramps and On-Ramps*.
12. Hewlett, *Off-Ramps and On-Ramps*, xi.
13. Nancy P. Rothbard and Lakshmi Ramarajan, "Checking Your Identities at the Door? Positive Relationship between Nonwork and Work Identities: Exploring Identities and Organizations," in *Exploring Positive Identities and Organizations: Building a Theoretical and Research Foundation*, ed. Laura Morgan Roberts and Jane E. Dutton (New York: Routledge, 2009). hbs.edu, http://www.people.hbs.edu/lramarajan/RothbardRamarajan.pdf.
14. Rothbard and Ramarajan, "Checking Your Identities," 127.
15. Rothbard and Ramarajan, "Checking Your Identities," 128.
16. Rothbard and Ramarajan, "Checking Your Identities," 128.
17. Anna Fels, *Necessary Dreams: Ambition in Women's Changing Lives* (New York: Pantheon Books, 2004).
18. Fels, *Necessary Dreams*, xx.
19. Betty Friedan, *The Feminine Mystique* (New York: W. W. Norton and Company, 1963).

20. Friedan, *The Feminine Mystique*, 75.
21. Robert Kegan and Lisa Laskow Lahey, *Immunity to Change: How to Overcome It and Unlock the Potential in Yourself and Your Organization* (Boston: Harvard Business Press, 2009).
22. Kegan and Laskow Lahey, *Immunity to Change*, 28, Figure 1.7.
23. Kegan and Laskow Lahey, *Immunity to Change*, 28, Figure 1.7.

2 A Simple Framework

1. Kripalu Center for Yoga and Health, kripalu.org, http://kripalu.org/.
2. Tanglewood Music Center, Boston Symphony Orchestra, http://www.bso.org/micro-sites/tanglewood-music-center/home.aspx.
3. Babson College, Center for Women's Entrepreneurial Leadership, babson.edu, http://www.babson.edu/Academics/centers/cwel/Pages/home.aspx; Susan Duffy, babson.edu, http://www.babson.edu/Academics/centers/cwel/about/team/Pages/duffy-susan.aspx.

3 Our Reactions

1. Sandy Anderson, *Women in Career & Life Transitions* (Indianapolis: JIST, 2000), 95.
2. Barbara Kivowitz, *In Sickness as in Health: Helping Couples Cope with the Complexities of Illness*, (Petaluma, CA: Roundtree Press, 2013).
3. Interview Barbara Kivowitz, November 24, 2014.
4. *The Diane Rehm Show*, "The Ongoing Struggle to Balance Career and Family, NPR, June 25, 2012, http://thedianerehmshow.org/shows/2012-06-25/ongoing-struggle-balance-career-and-family.
5. Carey Goldberg, "When You Lose Your Sport, What Happens To Your Self?" CommonHealth blog, WBUR, May 17, 2012, http://commonhealth.wbur.org/2012/05/former-athletes-group.

4 Is Transition Gendered?

1. Neil Aronson and Larry Gennari, galawpartners.com, http://www.galaw-partners.com/.
2. Route 128 Belt refers to MA Rt 128, a term often used to represent the high-technology industry that dotted the towns along its route. See "Massachusetts Route 128," *Wikipedia*, last modified July 3, 2015, http://en.wikipedia.org/wiki/Massachusetts_Route_128.
3. "Socialization," *Wikipedia*, last modified May 18, 2015, http://en.wikipedia.org/wiki/Socialization. Cross reference source, "Socialization," businessdirectory.com, http://www.businessdictionary.com/definition/socialization.html.

4. Lyn Mikel Brown and Carol Gilligan, *Meeting at the Crossroads: Women's Psychology and Girls' Development* (Cambridge, MA: Harvard University Press, 1992).
5. Mikel Brown and Gilligan, *Meeting at the Crossroads*, 3.
6. Mikel Brown and Gilligan, *Meeting at the Crossroads*, 2.
7. Mikel Brown and Gilligan, *Meeting at the Crossroads*, 3.
8. Mikel Brown and Gilligan, *Meeting at the Crossroads*, 217.
9. Mikel Brown and Gilligan, *Meeting at the Crossroads*, 229. Research conducted via a longitudinal study of second- through eleventh-grade girls at the Laurel School for girls in Cleveland, Ohio.
10. Mikel Brown and Gilligan, *Meeting at the Crossroads*, 202–203.
11. American Enterprise Institute, "Stunning College Degree Gap: Women Have Earned Almost 10 Million More College Degrees Than Men Since 1982," aei.org, http://www.aei.org/publication/stunning-college-degree-gap-women-have-earned-almost-10-million-more-college-degrees-than-men-since-1982/.
12. Adam Bryant, "Finding and Owning Your Voice," *New York Times*, Sunday Business Corner Office Column, November 13, 2014. nytimes.com, http://www.nytimes.com/interactive/2014/11/16/business/corner-office-women-executives-owning-their-voice.html.
13. TED Radio Hour, "The Haves and Have Nots," NPR, http://www.npr.org/2013/10/16/235781665/haves-and-have-nots.
14. TED Radio Hour, Jacqueline Novogratz, interview, "Is Patient Capital the Answer to Poverty?" NPR, http://www.npr.org/2013/10/18/235824059/is-patient-capitalism-the-answer-to-poverty.
15. Deborah Kolb, Judith Williams, and Carol Frohlinger, *Her Place at the Table* (San Francisco : Jossey-Bass, 2010).
16. Anna Fels, *Necessary Dreams* (New York: First Anchor Books, 2004), 94 and 95.
17. Fels, *Necessary Dreams*, 99.
18. Fels, *Necessary Dreams*, 47.
19. Fels, *Necessary Dreams*, 98.
20. Joan C. Williams, Reshaping the Work Family Debate: Why Men and Class Matter (Cambridge, MA: Harvard University Press, 2010).
21. Williams, *Reshaping the Work-Family Debate*, 78.
22. Sandra Lipsitz Bem, *The Lenses of Gender: Transforming the Debate on Sexual Inequality* (New Haven: Yale University Press, 1993).
23. Bem, *The Lenses of Gender*, 2.
24. Joan C. Williams, "Why Men Work So Many Hours," *Harvard Business Review: HBR Blog Network*, hbr.org, May 29, 2013, http://blogs.hbr.org/2013/05/why-men-work-so-many-hours/.
25. Williams, "Why Men Work So Many Hours." Italics added.
26. Williams, "Why Men Work So Many Hours."
27. Williams, "Why Men Work So Many Hours."
28. Claire Cain Miller and Liz Alderman, "Why US Women Are Leaving Jobs Behind," *The New York Times*, December 12, 2014, http://kff.org/other/poll

-finding/kaiser-family-foundationnew-york-timescbs-news-non-employed-poll/.

29. Claire Cain Miller and Liz Alderman, "Why US Women Are Leaving Jobs Behind," *The New York Times*, December 12, 2014, http://www.nytimes.com/2014/12/14/upshot/us-employment-women-not-working.html?abt=0002&abg=; Jess Bidgood, "Number of Mothers in U.S. Who Stay Home Rises," *The New York Times*, April 8, 2014, A15, http://www.nytimes.com/2014/04/09/us/number-of-stay-at-home-mothers-in-us-rises.html.

5   A Process Overview

1. Merriam-Webster, s.v. "hypothesis," http://www.merriam-webster.com/dictionary/hypothesis.
2. Stephen Levy, *In the Plex: How Google Thinks, Works and Shapes our Lives* (New York: Simon & Schuster, 2011).
3. *Renovation Raiders*, HGTV.com, http://www.hgtv.com/.
4. "Agile Software Development Methodology," *Wikipedia*, last modified July 10, 2015, http://en.wikipedia.org/wiki/Agile_software_development.
5. Clay Christensen, *The Innovator's Dilemma* (New York: Harper Collins Publishers, 1997).
6. Clay Christensen, James Allworth, and Karen Dillon, *How Will You Measure Your Life?* (New York: Harper Business, 2012), 87.
7. Christensen, Allworth, and Dillon, *How Will You Measure Your Life?*, 49.
8. Christensen, Allworth and Dillon, *How Will You Measure Your Life?*, 46.
9. Eleanor Roosevelt, *It's Up to the Women* (New York: Fredrick A. Strokes, 1933), 9.

6   Our First Steps

1. reacHIRE, http://www.reachire.com/.
2. Gail Sheehy, *Passages: Predictable Crises of Adulthood* (New York: Ballantine Books, 1974).
3. Sheehy, *Passages*, 499.
4. Adam Kahane, delivered at Fast Company's Real Time Conference in Orlando, FL, May 7, 2000, published as "How to Change the World: Lessons for Entrepreneurs from Activists," *Reflections*, 2, no. 3 (2001), by Generon Consulting, http://www.sonoraninstitute.org/images/stories/WLC/CBI_Workshop/Binder/gbn_kahane.savetheworld.pdf. Kahane worked at Royal Dutch Shell's Strategic Planning Department in London.
5. Malcolm Gladwell, "The Creation Myth, Xerox Parc, Apple and the Truth About Innovation," *The New Yorker*, May 16, 2011, http://www.newyorker.com/magazine/2011/05/16/creation-myth.
6. Kahane, "How to Change the World," 2.
7. Gail Rentsch, *Smart Women Don't Retire They Break Free* (New York: Spring Board Press, 2008), 67.

8. Dictionary.reference.com, s.v. "anagram," http://dictionary.reference.com /browse/anagram?s=t.

9. The Commonwealth Institute, http://commonwealthinstitute.org/.

10. Herminia Ibarra, *Working Identity: Unconventional Strategies for Reinventing Your Career* (Boston: Harvard Business School Press, 2003).

11. Ibarra, *Working Identity*, 121.

7   Reaching Forward

1. Terra Stanley, "The Ten Most Innovative Business School Courses," *Forbes*, August 9, 2010, http://www.forbes.com/2010/08/09/most-innovative -business-school-classes-entrepreneurs-management-sustainable-tech-10 -innovative.html. The piece features, Babson College's course as #7, "The Gig Economy and the New Entrepreneurial Imperative."

2. iRelaunch, http://www.irelaunch.com/.

3. "Psychological testing," Wikipedia, last updated May 25, 2015. https:// en.wikipedia.org/wiki/Psychological_testing

4. Barbara Kivowitz, *In Sickness as in Health: Helping Couples Cope with the Complexities of Illness* (Petaluma, CA: RoundTree Press, 2013).

5. Definition of networking provided by Google https://www.google .com/?gws_rd=ssl#q=definition+networking.

6. William Bridges, *Transition: Making Sense of Life's Changes* (Cambridge, MA: Da Capo Press, 1980), 17.

7. Six Sigma, iSixsigma.com http://www.isixsigma.com/tools-templates /cause-effect/determine-root-cause-5-whys/.

8   Barriers to Transition

1. Gloria Steinem, keynote speaker at The Commonwealth Institute's Breakfast of Champions, June 4, 2008. The Commonwealth Institute is a not-for-profit organization that helps women-led businesses get and stay successful. http://commonwealthinstitute.org/.

2. National Basketball Association, The Boston Celtics. http://www.nba.com /celtics/.

9   Getting Started

1. Anne D. LeClaire, *Listening Below the Noise: Meditation on the Practice of Silence* (New York: Harper, 2009).

2. LeClaire, *Listening Below the Noise*, 126.

3. Walter Isaacson, *Steve Jobs* (New York: Simon & Schuster, 2011).

4. Steve Jobs, "Commencement address" (Stanford University, Stanford, CA, June 12, 2005).

5. Jobs, "Commencement address."

6. Rainer Maria Rilke, from *Letters to a Young Poet: The Possibility of Being* (New York: MJF Books, 2002). Additional source: Awakin.org, http://www.awakin.org/read/view.php?tid=747. The expanded quote: "Don't search for the answers, which could not be given to you now, because you would not be able to live them. And the point is, to live. Everything. Live the questions now. Perhaps then, someday far in the future, you will gradually, without even noticing it, live your way into the answer."

7. Anne Crittenden, *The Price of Motherhood: Why the Most Important Job in the World Is Still the Least Valued* (New York: Henry Holt and Company, 2001).

8. Crittenden, *The Price of Motherhood*, 89.

9. Evelyn Murphy, with E. J. Graff, *Getting Even: Why Women Don't Get Paid Like Men and What To Do About It* (New York: Simon & Schuster, 2005).

10. Murphy, *Getting Even*, 26.

11. The Series 7 Exam administered by the Financial Industry Regulatory Authority (FINRA) allows those who pass to trade securities.

Index